Contents

MAKING EFFECTIVE PRESENTATIONS

Robert B. Nelson
Jennifer B. Wallick

The Scott, Foresman Applications
in Management Series

ROBERT B. NELSON, *Editor*

SCOTT, FORESMAN AND COMPANY
Glenview, Illinois   London

Library of Congress Cataloging-in-Publication Data

Nelson, Robert B.
　　Making effective presentations / Robert B. Nelson,
Jennifer Wallick.
　　　　p.　　cm. — (The Scott, Foresman applications in
management series)
　　　　ISBN 0-673-38956-1
　　　　1. Public speaking.　2. Business communication.
　　I. Wallick, Jennifer.　II. Title.　III. Series.
　　PN4121.N428　1990
　　808.5′1—dc20　　　　　　　　　　　　　　89-24224
　　　　　　　　　　　　　　　　　　　　　　　　　　CIP

1 2 3 4 5 6 RRC 94 93 92 91 90 89

ISBN 0-673-38956-1

Notice of Liability

Scott, Foresman professional books are available for bulk
sales at quantity discounts. For information, please
contact Marketing Manager, Professional Books Group,
Scott, Foresman and Company, 1900 East Lake Avenue,
Glenview, IL 60025.

Series Foreword

The Scott, Foresman Applications in Management Series provides short, practical, easy-to-read books about basic business skills.

Low on theory and high on practical techniques and examples, this series addresses the key skill areas needed to be a successful manager in business today. It supplies specific answers to questions you have and offers new approaches to problems you face in your job.

Each book in the series is written by one or more individuals who have extensive, firsthand experience in the topic being discussed. The drafted books are then reviewed by several front-line managers to assure that each meets their needs in delivering practical, useful information in a format that is easy to understand and use.

I am confident that this book—and others in the AIM series—will provide you with tips and techniques to enable you to do your job better today and in the future.

Robert B. Nelson
Series Editor

Acknowledgments

The authors would like to gratefully acknowledge the assistance and support of Roger Mosvick, Jim Regan, Barbara Braham, Amy Davis, Sandy Cherrey, and Al McCormick in the development of this book.

1

So You're Giving a Presentation . . .

Not very many people are born presenters. Speaking to a group is a learned skill that involves knowing how to prepare and practice so that your presentation flows smoothly and professionally—and accomplishes your objectives. If you're feeling nervous about your presentation, you are not alone! Public speaking is one of the most common fears that people have. You will find, however, that once you know how to prepare for and practice your presentation, your nervousness will diminish! You will also find that you can use your nervousness to your advantage when you deliver your presentation.

SPEAKING YOUR WAY
UP THE CAREER LADDER

Your ability to give oral presentations is your key to new opportunities in your life. You will face more and more opportunities to speak to groups as you move into positions of increased responsibility and expertise. Speaking to groups will be an integral part of your job if you plan ever to manage, lead, sell, or promote. Each speaking situation is an opportunity for you to display your expertise and to win others over to your way of thinking. It is an important skill worth mastering for many reasons.

Visibility in Your Organization

Consider your career in an organization. Rising to the top depends greatly on the right type of "visibility" with the right people. People need to know who you are and what you do—and giving oral presentations gives you the perfect opportunity to present your work and your professional skills. Your manager is going to have a much easier time getting your promotion approved when his or her manager knows who you are and what a great job you do. Presentations give you direct access to the managers of an organization and enable you to leave a favorable impression in a short amount of time. It is an established fact of life in organizations that those who present well, move well.

A Leadership Skill

If you want to develop your potential as a leader, you need a clear and powerful speaking style to motivate and inspire others. You need to be able to represent the views of others as well as yourself—

to be a spokesperson for a given cause. Your ability to give oral presentations can move you closer toward the goal of being an effective leader.

A Decision-Making Tool

One of the most common problems that organizations share is inaccurate communication within the organization. Organizations need people who can clearly communicate key information. A clear presentation keeps people in your organization well-informed and helps your organization make correct decisions. Your obligation to your employer is to make your ideas and recommendations clear and their consequences understandable.

These are a few of the reasons why effective communication is important to master. They add up to more than just getting through the speech your manager asked you to give. These reasons suggest that your ability to present is one of your most powerful professional skills.

COMMON MYTHS
ABOUT PRESENTATIONAL SPEAKING

If you are like most people, your mental image of public speaking has come from years of watching movies and listening to politicians give their campaign speeches. Let's start on the right track by getting rid of some of the most common misconceptions about presentational speaking.

Myth: Speakers Are Born, Not Made

Don't give up all hope of improving your own speaking skills when you see an accomplished speaker give an awesome and polished presentation! These speakers—political, military, church leaders, and so on—are so skilled that it seems their ability to communicate must be innate. This is seldom the case! Although upbringing and early exposure to speaking situations can have an influence on the level of skill and confidence of a speaker, it is never too late to learn the skills needed to be an effective communicator.

What you may not realize when you listen to a good presentation is how much work went into making that speech. Usually the speaker has given the same presentation a number of times. They have probably practiced the presentation five to six times, and probably were experts on the topic to begin with. Even a spontaneous presentation, in which the speaker is called on without previous notice to "say a few words," is a situation for which an experienced speaker has learned to prepare. The accomplished spontaneous speaker will choose from a number of "stock" presentations that he or she has effectively used in previous situations. The astute speaker also learns to effectively anticipate when he or she will be called on, and will be ready with possible topics and comments.

The point is, as with so many skills, an experienced person makes it look very easy when the novice knows for a fact it is not. Do not be deceived by your impressions! Most speakers went through the same fears and doubts and made the same mistakes you will make as you master this skill.

Even the Best Speakers Need to Prepare for and Practice Their Presentations.

Myth: You Should Copy Someone Else's Speaking Style

Hearing a speaking style that is unique and effective can be misleading for a novice speaker. First, there is the temptation to try to imitate or adopt the style in your own speeches. This seldom works, and when someone else's style is incorporated into your own, your speech tends to come off as insincere and unbelievable. Second, a speaking style that is entertaining and has a lot of flair may be very dramatic, but most of the time this kind of speech is not very effective in day-to-day business communications. Presentational speaking focuses on relaying essential information in a clear and effective manner. Very few business presentations, if any, will ever go down in history as memorable speeches, so the speaking style of a great public figure may not be the best model to adopt for your own.

Myth: You Never Overcome Stage Fright

Stage fright is the most common concern for speakers learning to give presentations. Most speakers experience stage fright in varying degrees. There is a common notion that once you have stage fright, it will plague you the rest of your life in any and all speaking situations. This belief helps to reinforce the "why-bother-to-try" attitude about presentational speaking. The fact is, even though experienced public speakers feel stage fright, these same individuals learn to use their anxiety to their advantage. They learn to control their symptoms at a manageable level and then to channel their anxious energy into enthusiasm and gestures that improve their presentation. Many experts agree that experiencing nervousness prior to a presentation can be advantageous for the speaker as well as for the speaking situation. A speaker who is nervous about speaking is more likely to go to extra lengths to prepare, practice, and double-check all arrangements. The speech is likely to be more dynamic and exciting because the speaker seems more alive. A speaker who isn't nervous often comes across as boring or uninteresting.

Experts agree that anxiety in speaking situations usually stems from a speaker wanting to do the best job possible, rather than from the speaker fearing the situation. Chances are you will always have some degree of performance anxiety as you strive toward more and more challenging opportunities. But relief comes in knowing that your object is not to rid yourself of this anxiety, but to learn to become comfortable with the feeling and to *use* it to enhance your personal speaking style.

Myth: Manuscript Speaking Is Better

This is a common myth. Our role models for speech delivery—TV newscasters, inaugural speeches, conference papers—all read from prepared manuscripts. While this may be a necessary or traditional mode of delivery for certain public presentations, it is not the acceptable mode of delivery for most business presentations. Manuscript speaking is an ineffective crutch for a new speaker and should be avoided at all costs. It is likely to smother your natural style and put your audience to sleep, because they will feel you are reading to them rather than communicating with them. It has the potential of being insulting as well as ineffective for relaying information.

Myth: Presentations Must Be Memorized to Be Effective

Memorizing a speech is ineffective because it gives you a mechanical, "canned" presentation style that is as offensive to your audience as being read to. Instead, the modern-day speaker should work from a few notes that outline the presentation. The delivery should be natural, as in a discussion. The main ideas and points to be communicated should be clear in your head, but the exact wording and delivery can vary with the specific occasion.

Myth: Presentations Must Be Formal to Be Effective

This is a common myth that is fostered by the fact that most of the time when we speak to a group, we are speaking to people we don't know very well. Since we may not know the people in the audience very well, or since the people in the audience might be important managers and decision-makers in the organization, we somehow decide that the speech should be "formal."

The problem with this myth is that if your personal style is not a formal one you will not feel at ease in the speaking situation. You will try to be something or someone you are not, and your delivery will feel and look awkward. More formal also often means more boring. Stale, lofty language coupled with a dry, monotonous tone are common characteristics of a formal delivery.

Informal presentations that are appropriate and well organized can be much more effective, for several reasons. For one, they are more interesting to listen to. An informal style will allow audience members to feel closer to the speaker, almost as if the presentation were directed specifically to each audience member. Another good reason for using informal deliveries is that they allow speakers to be themselves. If the speaker is comfortable, he or she will be more persuasive and sincere. Put aside all of these myths and remember:

- Good speakers are made, not born.
- Use your own speaking style.
- Stage fright can be used to your advantage.
- Don't read your speech.
- Don't memorize your speech.
- Presentations don't have to be formal.

WHAT YOU WILL LEARN FROM THIS BOOK

This book teaches you how to prepare and deliver an effective presentation—whether it is for three or three hundred people. This book uses five simple principles to turn you into an effective presenter.

One: Understand, Control, and Use Your Stage Fright

Understanding your stage fright is the first step toward controlling it. This book explores where your stage fright comes from and gives you a variety of techniques for controlling your symptoms of stage fright. This book also teaches you how to be well prepared for your presentation. You will find that many of your anxieties go away when you are prepared for your speech.

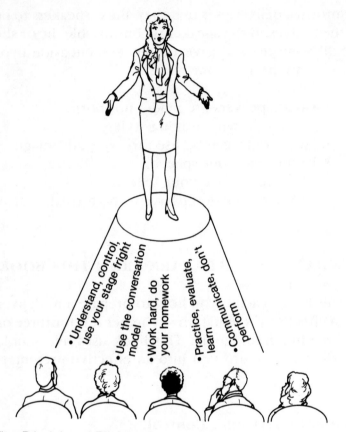

Five Principles of Effective Presentations.

Two: Work Hard and Do Your Homework

The fact of the matter is that almost anyone can become an excellent speaker given the proper instruction, attitude, and preparation. The magic as well as the apprehension about your presentation will fade as the reality of the task becomes clear. The reality of delivering a quality presentation is a step-by-step logical approach for preparing and practicing your presentation. This book gives you a step-by-step formula for (a) deciding what you want to say, and (b) determining how you want to say it.

Three: Communicate, Don't Perform

Although some forms of public speaking are entertaining and dramatic, this is not the case with most business presentations. The bottom line of an effective presentation is that the most vital information should be communicated in a clear manner that motivates the audience toward a specific objective. All of your preparation and delivery should support this goal, and overly dramatic or humorous styles, "canned" gestures or phrases, or other types of "acting" will distract your audience from your objective. A speaker may be able to keep an audience in stitches for twenty minutes, but if when done no one can remember what that person had to say, the speaker did not achieve his or her business objective.

Four: Use the Conversational Model

Normal conversation should be the model for both your verbal and nonverbal communication during a presentation. When you don't know what to say to a group, think about how you would explain the same information if you were talking to an individual. With a few adjustments, this will be the best first rule of thumb to guide you in developing your presentation. Think of your presentation as a one-on-one conversation in which you state your points in a clear, direct language. Continue to your next point when you perceive or sense that your audience understands your point. You can sense when the audience understands your point from the looks on their faces and from the nodding of their heads.

Pay attention to your nonverbal behavior during a presentation. Experts agree that your nonverbal behavior represents 60 percent to 90 percent of everything you communicate. Pay special attention to your eye contact. Make eye contact with your audience during a presentation in the same way that you would make eye contact during a one-on-one conversation. Our eyes serve as a "gatekeeper" to our thoughts. We use eye contact to signal when we have completed one thought and are about to begin another. The amount and type of eye contact you use is crucial for communicating the sincerity and honesty of your message.

Five: Practice, Evaluate, and Learn

To become a good public speaker you need to practice giving speeches and you need to evaluate your performance each time you give a speech. This book is filled with techniques and ideas to help you become a good public speaker. You'll find worksheets and checklists in this book that can be used to help you develop and practice your speeches. You will also find evaluation sheets to help you learn how to improve.

EVALUATING YOUR CURRENT SKILLS

Before you jump into the rest of this book, take some time right now to evaluate your current presentation skills. Research shows that any learning experience is more successful when the learner has preconceived ideas about what he or she would like to learn. This book will help you more if you know what specific areas of presentational speaking you need to improve.

What follows are two preliminary surveys, the first of which will help you take inventory of where you are in your speaking skills and where you would like to be. The second allows you to compare your self-perceptions with the qualities of a good public speaker.

TAKE YOUR SPEAKING INVENTORY

Self-Description.   Describe yourself as a speaker by selecting five descriptive words that come to mind (e.g., humorous, boring, etc.):

1. _____
2. _____
3. _____
4. _____
5. _____

Strengths.   List the characteristics that are your greatest assets in presentational speaking:

_____
_____
_____
_____

Weaknesses. List those areas that you have to improve to be better at presentational speaking:

_____

_____

_____

_____

Behavioral Goal. Describe how you would imagine yourself if you were effective at presentational speaking:

_____

_____

_____

_____

Knowledge Goal. List several specific questions that you would like answered before you have finished this book:

_____

_____

_____

_____

Commitment to Learning. What or how do you specifically stand to benefit by becoming more effective at presentational speaking?

_____

_____

_____

_____

SCORE YOURSELF AS A SPEAKER

For each question, circle one of the following letters that best represents your present status as a public speaker. Of course, this is just your own estimate of yourself and not a scientific test. Tally your score to find out how your characteristics rank against the characteristics of an accomplished public speaker.

1. When called upon unexpectedly to speak, do I?
   A. Get confused
   B. Keep cool and collected
   C. Have heart palpitation
   D. Have tongue stick
   E. Think well on my feet

2. What is my attitude while speaking?
   A. Worried
   B. Earnestly interested
   C. Contagiously enthusiastic
   D. Self-confident

3. About what have I the most speech information?
   A. My occupation
   B. My hobby
   C. My reading
   D. Personal experiences
   E. Church interests

4. What effect does my speaking have on the audience?

A. Usually boring
B. Tolerated
C. Persuasive
D. Convincing
E. Entertaining
F. Instructive

5. In preparing for a speech, do I?
   A. Gather and arrange ample material
   B. Rely on inspiration of occasion
   C. Jot down a few ideas

6. Is my memory of speech points?
   A. Poor
   B. Fair
   C. Good
   D. Excellent

7. In opening a talk, do I?
   A. Apologize
   B. Hem and haw
   C. Quickly catch favorable attention

8. Do my speeches?
   A. Have a pleasing closing
   B. Fizzle out and stop
   C. Result in favorable action by the audience

9. How is my platform presence?
   A. Slouchy
   B. Composed
   C. Ill at ease

10. How is my vocabulary?
    A. Too meager
    B. Ordinary
    C. Complete and accurate

11. How is my enunciation?
    A. Clear
    B. Mumbled or slurred
    C. Restrained behind tight lips

12. How do my ideas come out?
    A. Logically arranged
    B. Jumbled
    C. Fairly clear
    D. Psychologically effective

13. In speaking, do I think chiefly?
    A. Of myself
    B. Of the audience
    C. Of the words of my speech

14. How keen is my desire to speak in public?
    A. Rather have this ability than any other
    B. Wish I had the gift
    C. Would study half-hour daily for four
       months

TO SCORE your public speaking efficiency, add the figures assigned to each question. Par is 100; low score is 10.

1. A(0), B(6), C(2), D(0), E(8)
2. A(1), B(6), C(8), D(5)
3. A(5), B(5), C(5), D(5), E(5)

4. A(0), B(1), C(8), D(6), E(8), F(5)
5. A(8), B(0), C(3)
6. A(0), B(1), C(3), D(5)
7. A(1), B(0), C(8)
8. A(4), B(1), C(8)
9. A(0), B(5), C(1)
10. A(0), B(2), C(6)
11. A(8), B(0), C(1)
12. A(6), B(0), C(4), D(9)
13. A(1), B(6), C(3)
14. A(8), B(2), C(4)

2

Overcoming Your Initial Barrier: Stage Fright

You are not alone if you experience nervousness or anxiety before or during a presentation. It is a concern that needs to be addressed early in this book so that it will not haunt you during each step of your preparation. Let's focus first on understanding stage fright and then on overcoming, controlling, and utilizing your anxiety to your advantage.

UNDERSTANDING STAGE FRIGHT

Most speech counselors and instructors believe that stage fright stems from the prehistoric defense system of the human species. When early humans were faced with a perceived threat the physical reaction was that of "fleeing or fighting," and energy was directed toward one of those two ends. When we are faced with perceived threats in our modern world, we have the same reaction, yet neither fleeing nor fighting is an appropriate reaction to the speaking situation. We *can* avoid speaking situations (even if it isn't in our best interest). However, once we are standing in front of a group of people it is not appropriate to run out of the room. It is equally inappropriate to "fight" the audience, because they are seldom openly hostile and—thank goodness—never openly violent toward you as a speaker. What you are left with is an increased level of energy with only a few avenues for using it. If you don't direct this extra energy through the proper channels, your extra energy will "ooze out" in inappropriate and/or distracting ways.

What is it we fear? Why do we feel threatened when we speak to a group? We fear the situation because we are taking a risk. Even if we know the audience members well, and sometimes because we know the audience very well, the situation is fearful. We are on stage. Large numbers of people are evaluating us. We want people to like us. We are exposing our thoughts and beliefs in a short amount of time to a number of different individuals. We are risking our reputation with people we respect or with people above us in the organization, and the consequences seem enormous. If we fail, we will face many of the same individuals the next day or at the next performance review. Just as a successful presentation can have a positive impact on our career, a poor presentation can have a negative impact.

We fear the evaluation that others are making of us and we fear the potential for rejection. We fear

Stage Fright Stems from Our Prehistoric Defense Systems.

living up to the expectations of others. Because we fear the situation, we set tough expectations for ourselves. A slip of the tongue, a poor word selection, or a mispronounced word will be a major flaw to us when we are being hypercritical of ourselves—although such a slip will not even be noticed, much less remembered by members of the audience. Let's consider several aspects of stage fright that will help unravel some of the mysteries behind it.

Stage Fright Is Normal

You are abnormal if you don't feel anxious or nervous about your presentation. It is your body's way of alerting you to be prepared. The more important the situation is to you, the more stage fright you will experience. If you don't feel anxious about the presentation, then you probably won't have much energy or enthusiasm for the presentation. You won't prepare as well, you won't feel as excited about it, and you probably won't have as much energy when you deliver it. As a result you will come across as an unprepared, boring speaker to your audience. Speakers who aren't anxious about their presentation run the risk of being inappropriate, offending the audience, using humor in bad taste, or rambling on—oblivious to the audience's reaction. So stage fright really has a positive impact on your public speaking! You'd be much worse off if you weren't fearful of the situation. Be glad you are anxious about your presentation and learn to use your anxiety to your advantage!

Stage Fright Seems More Severe to the Speaker

When you are onstage, your symptoms of stage fright are amplified, especially when you are looking for them. Very few of your stage fright symptoms will be detected by audience members, and those symptoms that are detected by the audience rarely detract from your presentation. An important thing to remember is that the audience is almost always on your side. The audience wants you to give a winning presentation! Most everyone in the audience understands stage fright—and will overlook symptoms of stage fright. Unfortunately, what usually happens is that a speaker will notice, for example, that his or her voice is cracking, and will think it is noticeable to the audience. This will make the speaker more uneasy, causing his or her voice to crack even more, and new symptoms of stage fright will appear. This cycle has the potential of escalating to the point where the speaker feels unable to continue. Members of the audience probably didn't think twice when the speaker's voice cracked. It was the speaker who escalated a small symptom of stage fright into a major problem.

Stage Fright Escalates the More You Seek to Escape It

One of the ironies about stage fright is that the more you try to avoid it, the more you are likely to experience it. People often come to fear the feeling of fear itself. Instead of trying to hide from fear in a speaking situation, you need to become comfortable with being uncomfortable. You need to accept the feeling of fear as being legitimate and be confident that it will quickly pass. You need to ignore negative symptoms and seek positive reinforcement from yourself or from others. You must come to a truce with fear rather than fight a battle you cannot win.

Stage Fright Symptoms Seem More Severe to the Speaker.

OVERCOMING STAGE FRIGHT

Preparation and Practice are the two most important techniques for overcoming stage fright. When you prepare well for your presentation, many anxieties and "what ifs" will be eliminated and you will feel much more confident when you give your presentation. Some experts suggest that as much as 75 percent of speech anxiety can be avoided through adequate preparation. If you know what you are going to say ahead of time, and have practiced the speech, you will feel more comfortable when you deliver your presentation. Making the time to prepare for your presentation may be easier said than done, but it is worth it. Make it a priority to prepare for and practice your presentation!

Let's look at some specific approaches for overcoming stage fright. Different techniques will work best for different people.

Aware-Accept-Act

The aware-accept-act (AAA) technique uses a simple, three-step formula to cope with your stage fright.

Become Aware. The first step is to be aware of what is happening to you when you become fearful. Once you are sensitized to your level of fear, it will be easier for you to stop your fear from escalating. Even panic, which occurs without warning, can be curtailed when you recognize what is happening to you. Pay attention to physical symptoms like your breathing pattern or your muscle tension. Your body will tell you how nervous or relaxed you feel.

Accept the Emotion. Once you are able to sense when you are scared, you need to learn to accept the emotion as being valid—and quit feeling guilty or foolish or inferior because of it. It is perfectly natural to be anxious in speaking situations. To deny that this is normal, or say that it should not be happening to you, is going to make you more fearful and it will be harder for you to handle your fear. Instead, when fear comes, welcome it! Consider it a form of energy that can motivate you to better prepare prior to a presentation and make you a more enthusiastic speaker during your presentation. Treat it as an ally that can make you a better speaker.

Act on It. After you are aware of and accept fear, all you need to do is act on it. Do something different! Do not become a passive recipient of a feeling you dread. If you don't know what to do to curb your fear, try any different behavior! With some experience, you will be able to identify more specifically what action curtails your fear.

If you don't take aggressive actions to counter your fear, your fear will grow and paralyze you. If you simply stand there as you feel fear set in, you will feel more and more uncomfortable. The longer you wait, the harder it will be to combat the emotion. Take charge of your fear!

An Example of Using AAA. I want to share an example from my life where I've seen AAA control stage fright. My boss and I were giving a presentation to a group of 250 people at a conference. My boss was doing the first half of the presentation and I was doing the last half. It was my first conference presentation, and needless to say, I felt nervous. We were giving the talk on a product we had developed. My boss's part of the presentation was to survey products that were similar to ours and to emphasize the pitfalls of the competitors' products. My job was to describe why our product was so wonderful.

After the host introduced us, my boss walked up to the podium, put on his microphone, and started showing his viewgraphs, which summarized the advantages and disadvantages of the other products. Meanwhile, I was in my chair thinking, "Oh my God, I'm going to have to speak into a *microphone!*" The third viewgraph my boss put up talked about one of the most popular of competitor's products. My boss described the advantages and the disadvantages of the product, and then proceeded to crumple up the viewgraph, saying that the product was no good, and to throw the crumpled-up viewgraph into the audience. Everybody laughed when he threw the viewgraph into the audience—it was such an unconventional thing to do—and yet it made his point. He broke the ice with the audience. I saw that the stage fright he had felt up to that point had gone away, and that the audience was anxious to hear more from us. He broke the ice for me too—I suddenly felt more relaxed about my own part of the presentation. It was a little trick that made such a big difference for both of us!

It was at this point that my boss taught me an important lesson about presentations. Whether the crumpled-up viewgraph was planned or spontaneous I'll never know. But I did see how it eased his stage fright and my own. For my own presentations, it doesn't fit my style to crumple up viewgraphs and throw them into the audience, but I do keep a bag of tricks ready when I feel my nervousness building. One of the things I find helps me the most when I feel my anxiousness building up is to have some kind of interaction with the audience. Usually, if the group is under fifty people, I will ask them a question and get some kind of response from them. This helps me to relax. I've also found that I feel more at ease during my presentations if I have talked to some members of the audience just prior to the presentation.

You need to find out which tricks work best for you when you start feeling nervous. Remember, the first thing you need to do is to realize *when* you are feeling nervous. Then you need to realize that it is OK to feel nervous. Finally, *channel* your nervousness into some kind of action (like a crumpled-up viewgraph) that helps you alleviate your nervous energy.

Rational Emotive Theory

Rational emotive theory, first developed by Robert Ellis, states that you can control your emotions, including fear and anxiety, through your thoughts. The crux behind this theory is that you can prepare and deliver a winning presentation by thinking through the situation ahead of time. To use the rational emotive theory to deal with your fear of speaking, do the following.

Imagine the Worst Case Scenario. Imagine the worst thing that could happen to you in your speaking situation. Take your analysis to an extreme. Perhaps the audience will criticize you, or maybe they'll laugh at you. Or maybe they will be so disgusted by your delivery that they will start to ignore you and leave the room. Your manager might become so outraged that he fires you—in front of the group! You might become so stressed that you have a heart attack and die on the spot!

Estimate the Chances of It Happening. Now, of all the negative consequences that could occur as a result of your presentation, what are the chances that any or all of them will actually materialize? When you really think about it, the chances of any of the negative consequences actually happening are very small.

Picture What Is Likely to Happen. Now, with the worst case scenarios out of the picture, imagine what is more likely to occur in your speaking situation and what specific problems might realistically arise. Think about some of the tough questions people might ask you. What if you can't answer a question? What if your voice cracks? What if you can't remember what you were going to say?

Minimize Potential Problems. Decide what you can do to minimize the chances of not being able to handle specific problems that are likely to come up. Resolve not to worry about those aspects of the situation that you don't have any control over.

This theory helps change blind fear into a tangible, rational process that can be examined and discussed. By doing so, the mystery of the unknown disappears and your energy can be directed toward actions that will do the most good.

An Example of Applying the Rational Emotive Theory. Let's walk through an example of how you can use the rational emotive theory and think through a speaking situation ahead of time to eliminate potential problems and reduce your fear of the situation. Suppose you have been under contract for the past year to do some work for a customer. You are now traveling to the customer's facility to give a status update on the project—and hopefully to get him or her to sign off on more money for the project for the upcoming year. The customer will have seven to twelve people listening to your presentation. Your job in your presentation is to let them know how things have been going for the past year, and to explain reasons as to why they should continue to fund your work.

1. *Imagine the Worst Case Scenario.* You give the presentation. Because you gave such a lousy presentation, your customer is convinced you are wasting their money and cancels your contract. Your boss fires you.

2. *What Are the Chances of This Really Happening?* You know that your group has been working hard for this customer and has produced some valuable results. So if you simply present your achievements over the past year (even if you are incredibly nervous during the presentation), it is very unlikely that the customer will think you have been wasting their money. There is always a chance that the customer might cancel the contract, but if you prepare well for your presentation the contract won't get canceled because the customer thinks you have wasted their money over the past year. In addition, your boss knows how hard you have worked on this project, and you have kept him or her informed along the way, so there is no real

chance that your boss would fire you because of this presentation.

3. *Picture What Is Likely to Happen.* When you really sit down and think about it, you believe that your customer will fund you for future work no matter how your presentation goes. The customer might want to have some impact on the directions you take, but you really feel that this person wants you to do the work. You'll be surprised at how much pressure gets released when you rule out those fears that are not likely to come true.

4. *Minimize Potential Problems.* Your presentation is really a three-part presentation. In the first part, you will be giving an overview of what progress you've made toward your goals. In the second part of the presentation, you will be giving a live demonstration of the work you have produced. And in the last part of the presentation, you will talk about your plans for the future.

So what can you do to minimize problems in each of these three areas? The following is a list of suggestions for minimizing problems in each of these areas:

One: Minimize Problems with the Status Update

a. Make sure your presentation reviews the initial goals of the project and illustrates how you have met these goals.

b. Emphasize how you have met each of the deadlines. If there were deadlines you were unable to meet, describe what problems came up that prevented you from meeting those deadlines.

c. Emphasize what results you have had from the project.

d. If applicable, emphasize areas where work was done that was above and beyond the call of duty.

e. Make a list of the tough questions they might ask you. How would you answer each of these questions?

Two: Minimize Problems with the Live Demonstration

a. Have backup plans ready in case something doesn't work or something isn't available. Videotape the demonstration if possible, and make sure your customer's facility has the right type of videotape player!

b. Make a list of the tough questions you might be asked. How would you answer each of these questions.

Three: Minimize Problems with Future Work Presentation

a. Try and view it from the customer's perspective. What are his or her needs, and how will your work solve any problems? What particular advantages can your company offer the customer? What particular expertise does your company have that others might not have?

b. Make a list of the tough questions they might ask you. How would you answer each of these questions?

All of these questions will help you prepare and plan a good presentation. If you have the tough questions answered ahead of time, you will feel more confident when you give your presentation. One other thing you might want to do now is to address some problems related to your actual delivery of the presentation:

a. What's my backup plan if I blank out while I'm giving the presentation? (Consult your notes.)

b. What will I do if my voice cracks? (Take a sip of water—make sure you have some there!)

c. What will I do if I start feeling really nervous? (Ask the audience a question: How many of you have heard of . . .?)

Remember, the idea behind the rational emotive theory is to work through the issues and potential problems associated with your speech ahead of time—that way you won't have very many surprises, and you will be prepared for those problems that do come up!

Systematic Desensitization

Systematic desensitization also uses your imagination to confront both the fear and the situation of speaking. It has proven to be one of the most effective methods for helping people who experience extreme anxiety about presentational speaking.

With this method, you shut your eyes and attempt to mentally walk through the stressful situation from its earliest conception to its final completion. Whenever you feel stress, you stop the exercise and attempt it again at a later time. No analysis is made as to why the fear exists or why it goes away. You repeat this exercise until you can mentally enact the entire speaking situation and associated behavior—such as the speech preparation—without experiencing physical anxiety.

A different approach that uses the same theory involves learning to face other intangible fears. Practice controlling your fright in situations where you know that there is no physical harm that can come to you. A good example is watching a scary movie. You know that the threat is imagined, yet the symptoms you experience are very real. A scary movie serves as an ideal situation to analyze and practice controlling your fear—facing your fear in order to be better able to work with it.

Go to a scary movie and, as you are watching, become aware of what your body is doing. Is your body squirming? Sit erect, facing the screen full front. Is your heart pounding? Close your eyes and consciously take longer and deeper breaths. Continue breathing in this deliberate manner as you watch. Experiment with giving yourself suggestions.

Try Going to a Scary Movie and Notice What Symptoms of Fear You Feel. What Can You do to Reduce or Control Those Symptoms?

"This is not that scary." "This is only a movie." "I am completely relaxed." "The music is scarier than the visual." See which suggestions are the most effective in diminishing your symptoms of fear, and remember them so that you can use them in those "fearful nightmares" of public speaking.

By doing this type of exercise, you are learning how to control irrational feelings in a rational way. You are using your ability to think, to anticipate and overpower your emotions when they are not serving constructive purposes. Many times we do not want to control our emotions. For example, if we are angry and feel we have a right to be angry, we may prefer to vent and display that anger. But it is still a valuable skill to know how to avoid or contain our anger in situations in which it is inappropriate. Establish the point at which fear becomes counterproductive for you if left unchecked. Learn how to contain or diminish that fear.

Hypnosis

Another method you can use to overcome stage fright is hypnosis. This method typically combines visual imagery to specifically identify what you fear in a speaking situation. With that information, you and the hypnotist design suggestions to help you at the specific moment of anxiety. These suggestions might consist of affirmations or other positive statements that would boost your confidence or serve as reminders of specific alternatives that are available to you when you become anxious. With repetition over several weeks, usually with the aid of a tape recorder, you will be able to integrate the new suggestions into your mental and behavioral responses to speaking situations. Hypnosis is also possible without the aid of a hypnotist. There are several books available on the topic of self-hypnosis. One I recommend is *Self Hypnotism: The Technique and its use in Daily Living,* 1964, Prentice-Hall, Englewood Cliffs, New Jersey, 17632.

These methods—aware-accept-act, rational emotive theory, systematic desensitization, and hypnosis—represent the most effective techniques known for overcoming stage fright in presentational speaking situations. By using these techniques, you will become skilled at managing your level of anxiety and redirecting the normal surge of energy that comes with speaking situations into channels that enhance rather than detract from your presentation. Arm gestures, body motion, and enthusiasm can become the acceptable outlets for your nervous energy that will improve your presentation style and effectiveness.

HANDLING SPECIFIC SYMPTOMS OF STAGE FRIGHT

When you are giving a presentation, you may feel nervous and display various symptoms of anxiety. If left unchecked, these symptoms are likely to increase in intensity and number and will be disruptive to your thinking and delivery. Here are some techniques that you can have in your hip pocket in the event of an anxiety attack prior to or during your presentation. Knowing that you have alternatives such as these will enable you to feel more confident and prepared. You always have alternatives in a speaking situation, including the choice to ignore a symptom.

Fear manifests itself in a wide variety of physiological symptoms. These symptoms can cause you to panic or, at the very least, can distract you or the audience from the presentation. Here are some of the most common symptoms of stage fright and some techniques for controlling and redirecting them so that they will not add to your fear or detract from your delivery.

Speechlessness

Warm up your voice prior to entering the speaking environment, and perhaps even hum in a low tone to yourself while you are waiting to start. Repeat to yourself the first words of your presentation. If you become speechless in the middle of your talk, stop and accept the feeling, take a breath, and then begin again. Focus on the face of a friend in the audience and imagine that you are talking to just one person.

Racing

If your reaction to fear is at the other extreme, and you progressively talk faster and faster, pause a moment so that you can gain control of your speed. If your heart is pounding and your head is swimming, again pause, close your eyes, and take a deep breath. Your intent is to try to limit the stimuli that are overexciting you. Imagine a peaceful scene or something you especially like, such as a favorite pastime or a person you admire. Stopping and redirecting your thoughts will redirect your behavioral response as well. Try using reminders to yourself in the margin of your notes, such as the words "slow down," or arrange to have an audience member give you a signal if you begin to talk too fast. Practice pauses so as to be comfortable with silence, and be especially sure that you deliver your key points such as the introduction, transitions, and closing, more loudly and more slowly.

Headaches

Any physical symptom prior to, during, or after a presentation is most likely a direct result of excessive tension. For example, one type of headache is caused by having your back muscles tighten so much that your scalp is pulled taut, resulting in painful pressure. Another common speaking headache occurs from not eating because your appetite is diminished due to anxiety. In the former case, take some aspirin on a preventative basis; in the latter case, eat something, however little—such as a bag of peanuts—to give your body needed energy.

Stiff or Shaky Muscles

This is a physiological symptom that is a carryover of our primitive "fight or flight" instinct. Remember, the mind does not distinguish between real and imagined fear; the body gets the same instructions either way. Your muscles are tensed and prepared for action.

When your muscles become extremely tense they start to shake, just the way your arm shakes when you try to squeeze an object very hard. Stiff muscles can cause a very rigid and animated delivery. They can hamper your ability to speak. Muscle tension can cause white-knuckle gripping of the lectern. The muscle tension may be focused, but it runs throughout your system, naturally affecting the very sensitive vocal muscles and respiratory muscles. You can't help it; if your body is too tense, your voice will give you away. Your voice is a marvelously sensitive barometer of your feelings—you must learn to make it work for you, not against you. It is difficult to effectively change your voice; it is much easier to change your feelings about making the speech.

There are a few techniques that can help you. First, learn to identify exactly which muscles are the most tense. These are the sets of muscles where your tension is focused and you can identify a distinct manifestation of tension. This is not as easy as it sounds. Your mind is on many other things while you are in a speaking situation, and you will have to pause to think about where the tension is in your body. Shaky or tense muscles may show up as a shaky hand or wobbly knees. The harder you try to control these muscles, the worse it gets. Once you isolate the tension, there are a number of ways to remove it. It is often effective to "shake off" the energy in tense muscles, particularly in the case of those telltale hands, before you begin. You may also try walking around briskly. Consciously tensing specific muscles as hard as possible and then quickly relaxing your control is another effective method. The key is to move the muscles that are tense. For example, a stiff front torso can often be relaxed by bending at the waist, perhaps to pick up an object, to break the rigid body armor.

Do not let your presentation make your shaking more apparent. If your hands are shaky, do not hold up any visual aids or point to items on a board or overhead projector. Likewise, if your knees are shaky, you may want to start speaking while leaning against or sitting on the edge of a table. Do not feel you are locked into having to speak from one specific location, even if a podium is present.

Shortness of Breath

Not having enough air to finish a sentence and not being able to take a complete breath are both caused by excessive muscle tension around your chest and stomach regions. Taking a deep breath and stretching your arms will help to break the chest tension, and at the same time will give you maximum air volume. Another trick is to make yourself yawn. You do this by taking in a series of breaths and trying to maintain them in the back of your throat. If you are unable to create a yawn at will, pay attention to what you feel the next time your body has a natural yawn. With practice you can then recreate the sensation at will. Naturally, you get all of this out of your system before you go in front of the group.

If you find you have become or are becoming short of breath, simply stop and take a deep breath. Take a moment between sentences or phrases to catch your breath and reestablish a natural speaking rhythm. If you don't, you will begin to breathe more and more shallowly as you keep talking. This will cause you to break sentences with unnatural pauses and will make what you are saying inaudible beyond a short distance. Pausing while taking a deep breath will allow you time to think about what you want to say next. This is very forgivable to the audience. If you feel uncomfortable stopping, give your audience a disclaimer such as: "Let me take a second and catch my breath, I'm starting to get ahead of myself." Most likely, this will make you come across as very excited about your topic, which can be a very positive feature of your presentation.

Excessive Sweating

Becoming flushed or warm because of anxiety often makes people sweat excessively. This visible sweat on the forehead, around the neck, in the palms of the hands, or from the armpits is beyond your control. The less you worry about it, the better it will be.

However, you can minimize the embarrassment by planning ahead. Have a handkerchief available and don't be shy about mopping your brow. Your audience will understand; after all, aren't you working very hard on their behalf? Loosen your tight-fitting collar prior to speaking, and if you wear glasses, dab some cornstarch on the nose bridge to avoid slippage. Wear a white shirt or blouse if you are prone to wetness under your arms, or simply avoid removing your jacket. You can usually make sure that a glass of water is near the lectern before you begin to speak. In extreme cases, rashes may develop. These will go away when the perceived threat of speaking is over.

Dry Mouth

The opposite reaction to excessive sweating is dehydration. A dry mouth or "cotton mouth" can be uncomfortable and also can affect your ability to pronounce words and speak clearly. If you are prone to this symptom, have a glass of water handy.

Pounding Heart

This symptom is your body's way of preparing you for quick defensive action. We seldom need this "fight or flight" energy today, although the extra energy can help us to be mentally alert. The pounding sound in your ears can be distracting, but of course this pounding cannot be heard by anyone else. Take long, slow breaths when you feel a rush of anxiety prior to and during a presentation, to help slow your heart down. In extreme cases, holding a long, deep breath will also help. Holding a long breath will decrease the amount of oxygen available to your blood and will slow down your pounding heart.

Cracking Voice

Excessive tension can show quickly in your voice. It usually comes from having tense neck muscles or an inadequate air supply to support your voice. Stretch your neck, clear your throat, and take a deep breath to counteract the effects of this symptom. Pause a moment and have a sip of water.

Shifting or Rocking Body Movements

Another outlet for nervous energy is excessive body movements. Any type of mannerism will distract from your communication and should be avoided.

Focus on keeping your weight on the balls of your feet and on keeping your body "dead" from the waist down. Planting your feet in this manner when you start speaking will encourage nervous movements to be translated into upper body gestures. Likewise, this stance will help keep you from leaning on a lectern too much. If your hands feel awkward and unnatural at your side, try placing one in your pocket and holding the other bent in front of you. This is preferable to gripping a lectern that is in front of you and not removing your grip until you are finished speaking.

Loose Change

Hands in the pockets can be annoying to an audience if you are playing with change or keys. It also restricts the use of arm gestures and thus is likely to make you less effective. Try standing with one arm bent in front of you and the other arm at your side. If you do have a tendency to slip a hand into your pocket, use a change purse to be sure that the pocket you slip your hand into is empty.

Twitches

Irregular muscle spasms or mannerisms can be difficult to control, but at the very least, be aware of them so that you can try different ways to stop them. Rubbing the muscle or stretching it may help, or turning that side of your body or face away from the audience may help make a twitch less conspicuous.

"Aaahs" and "Ummmms"

Possibly one of the most difficult mannerisms to correct is the verbal crutch of saying "ah" during a pause in your speech. When excessive, these faults can distract an audience. Practice speaking more deliberately with intentional pauses, always thinking before you speak. Listen to the sound or your own voice and be aware when your use of the language is becoming sloppy. This trait is usually found with hesitant speakers who are unsure of exactly what they want to say. It will typically diminish with practice.

Blanking Out

Sometimes you might just forget what you were going to say when you are giving a presentation. This symptom can devastate most speakers, although it doesn't seem to devastate us in one-on-one situations. When speaking with just one other person, we seldom are devastated when we lose our train of thought. It is quite natural to simply say, "What was I saying?" Likewise, when you are speaking to a group you can easily pause and refer to your notes, or ask, "I lost my train of thought, what was I saying?" Or, if the group is too large to ask or obtain assistance from anyone, simply continue with another point that strikes you as being important at that time: "That example will come to me, but meanwhile, one point I haven't emphasized is . . ." The extra moment that either of these alternatives provides will give you time to regain your composure.

Plan to have a strategy for when you blank out during your presentation. Regardless of the cause of the distraction, here are some specific techniques that you can adapt to your own style and use as needed:

Acknowledge You Forgot. As in a conversation, say: "That point momentarily escapes me," and continue on, "but let's look at the other reasons why . . ."

Fill in the Gap. Summarize, repeat the last point, restate your thesis, give a personal example. These will all give you time to remember where you were.

Shift the Attention. Ask for questions, poll the group on their opinion or an alternative for what to do next, or take a five-minute break. Remember that no one knows the agenda for your presentation except you!

Refer to Your Notes. As unobtrusively as possible, glance at your next point. Feel comfortable with the moment or two of silence. Use the silence as a means to emphasize your next point.

Summarize and Stop. If close to the end of your talk, this can be a good alternative.

Have a Catchall Phrase. Have a line to say that makes you feel comfortable regardless of the situation. "It seems like I'm getting ahead of myself; let me take a second and catch my breath." Having catch phrases will keep you from feeling helpless in a moment of panic. It will give you confidence that you have prepared for the worst and have several alternatives from which to choose should that happen.

With the techniques described in this chapter, you should now be equipped with many effective methods for overcoming, controlling, and redirecting stage fright in presentational speaking situations. By learning and practicing these techniques you will become skilled at managing your level of anxiety and redirecting nervous energy into channels that enhance rather than detract from your presentation. Arm gestures, body movements, and vocal enthusiasm can become the acceptable outlets for your energy and will also serve to enhance your presentational style and effectiveness.

A final thought regarding conquering any anxiety or fear you might have about presentational speaking is to take an aggressive attitude about speaking. The first moment that you are asked to give a presentation, respond in a positive way with "I'd be honored!" This will help to establish a positive, productive attitude toward that specific presentation, and you will be less likely to avoid, dread, or procrastinate on your preparation for the task. Keep in mind that a confident, aggressive approach to presentational speaking will keep most imagined fears from becoming a reality!

3

Planning Your Presentation

Now it's time to do your homework and plan your presentation! When you deliver your presentation you'll be glad for every minute you spent planning it.

Planning your presentation doesn't mean coming up with an outline—that comes in the next chapter on *preparing* your presentation. Planning your presentation means you need to

- Decide *what* the purpose of your presentation is;
- Analyze *who* your audience is;
- Think about *where* you will be giving your presentation;
- Jot down and prioritize all the ideas you have for your presentation.

What this really means is that you need to take a few moments and think about your speaking situ-

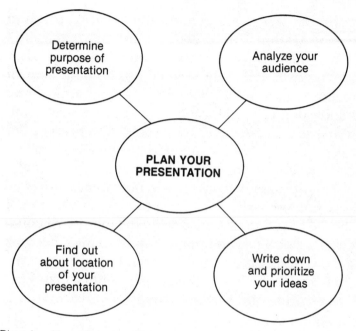

Planning Your Presentation.

ation. Let's look at a couple of examples of why assessing your speaking situation ahead of time is so important.

Example One: Planning Lets You Know What to Expect

Planning helps you know what to expect when you deliver your presentation. Consider the story of a marketing director of a large insurance brokerage firm in Cleveland, Ohio, who was asked to present to the municipal council her company's competitive bid for a group-benefits contract for employees. She accepted the assignment readily and felt that the opportunity was not only flattering but also critical to her professional progress.

When she arrived at the meeting hall, however, she discovered that the council was holding an open meeting. Along with its members were almost one hundred interested local citizens and municipal employees. Panic-stricken, she refused to present her case. She could not stand before such a large group and present her material clearly and convincingly.

This speaker had not done her homework. She was not prepared for her speaking situation. She should have called someone on the municipal council ahead of time and found out how many (and what groups of) people would be attending her presentation. She could have then prepared herself and her presentation for a larger group.

Example Two: Planning Ensures That Your Presentation Is on Target and Goes Smoothly

Assessing your speaking situation ahead of time assures you that your presentation is on target and that your delivery goes smoothly. Consider the following, which happened to a friend of mine.

Lisa worked for a research group in a major computer company. She had been working on a contract with the Army for a year. It was time to go back to the Army and give them a status update on the project. The presentation was to include a live demonstration of the work completed in the past year. Lisa generally knew who would be attending the presentation, so she prepared her slides and packed up a computer to ship on the plane. Lisa even made a videotape of the demonstration in case something went wrong with the computer and she could not give a live demonstration.

The Army's agenda involved a status review in the morning, a demonstration promptly after lunch, and a presentation of future work with the Army in the afternoon. As it turned out, some cables needed to be run for the computer, so while the morning group was giving their presentation, people were running around trying to hook up the computer. Of course, as Murphy's law dictates, when they finally hooked up the computer, it didn't work, and hence the live demonstration wasn't possible. Well, that was OK, because Lisa had brought a videotape of the live demonstration. Murphy was at it again, because the tape Lisa had brought was a VHS tape, and the Army only had Beta machines at that particular site. So much for any type of demonstration of the work that the Army had funded for the past year.

The day only got worse after this point, because Army management had recently changed and the Army was shifting its focus—and didn't want to fund any more work in this particular area. The whole three-year project was cancelled—after only one year. Oh well . . . chalk the whole trip up to experience.

Lisa came across two surprises in this presentation that could have been avoided with proper planning. First, she found out she wasn't going to be able to show the Army her demonstration of the work done to date; and second, she had no idea that some of the key players in charge of the project had changed. Better planning would have helped Lisa's presentation. At a very minimum, she should have called ahead to find out what kind of video machines the Army had at their facility. If the Army couldn't get a VHS machine, Lisa could have arranged for one to be there. With even more research, she could have found out that the Army was shifting the focus of their research, and she could have targeted her presentation on future work in the direction that the Army was taking.

Besides helping you to avoid surprises in your presentation, planning your presentation gives you a mechanism for breaking the ice on preparing your presentation. I have found that once I start answering questions about who is going to be in the audience, and at what facility I will be speaking, I lose any mental blocks I had about preparing my presentation. So let's now look at a formula for planning your presentation.

DEFINING YOUR PURPOSE

Clarity of thought is a prerequisite to clarity of communication. The first thing you need to do is to sit back and decide what the real purpose of your presentation is. Your presentation needs a clearly defined purpose. In particular, you need to answer the following questions.

- Why are you communicating information to this specific group?
- What do you hope to gain from the interaction?
- How will audience members benefit from what you have to say?
- Why wouldn't it be more beneficial to put the information in written form and distribute it?

To help you clarify the purpose of your presentation, let's first look at some of the most common categories of purposes that people have when they give a presentation. Once you have read them over, you will probably be able to classify the purpose of your presentation into one or more of these common categories. Once you have classified the purpose of your presentation, then we will examine how to write your statement of purpose for your presentation.

Classify Your Purpose

Most people, when they give a presentation, want to inform, persuade, and/or entertain their audience. Chances are likely that you can classify your purpose into one or more of these three categories. The format of your presentation will vary according to how you classify the purpose of your presentation. Let's look briefly at what your presentation needs to include if you want to inform, persuade, and/or entertain your audience.

To Inform Your Audience. Maybe the purpose of your presentation is to increase the audience's awareness about a specific topic. Presentations that inform include project status reviews and technical presentations at conferences. An informational presentation increases the audience's level of awareness regarding the topic, or gives the audience information that they might use to perform some activity. When you inform the audience about a topic, you need to be aware of how much people in the audience already know about it and you need to move them to a new level of awareness.

To Persuade Your Audience. Maybe you want your presentation to persuade the audience to think or act differently. The change you want from the audience might be a general one, such as a change of attitude regarding the role of the federal government in foreign affairs, or it may be a one-time occurrence, such as persuading a group to make a specific purchase. In either case, your presentation not only must give the audience members information that they do not already have but must motivate them to make use of that information.

To Entertain Your Audience. At a social affair, after dinner, or at a celebration, the purpose of your presentation might be less serious. Your presentation may be meant to only amuse and entertain the audience. This type of presentation calls for a special style of delivery and preparation.

Now, using these three categories, how would you classify your presentation? Take a minute to think it over and then write down which category or categories you think apply to your presentation.

Write Your Statement of Purpose

Once you have generally classified the purpose of your presentation into the appropriate category or a combination of categories, write out a single state-

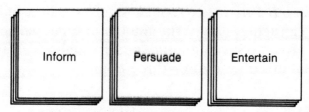

How Would You Classify the Purpose of Your Presentation?

ment that describes what you hope to achieve from your communication. This will serve to guide you through most of the decisions you will make while you prepare your speech. Using the following guidelines when you write your statement of purpose.

Make It Active. Use clear verbs and describe, from the recipient's point of view, what should happen:

- To be able to use the new accounting procedures.
- To purchase a six-month's supply of our industrial cleaner.

Be Specific. To help keep the purpose focused, use specific language and state what will be different. For example:

- To be able to reduce errors by over 20 percent within the next quarter.
- To identify five areas for potential cost savings.

Provided that your goal is reasonably attainable, this will enable you to quantify the effectiveness of your presentation.

Keep It Feasible. You must evaluate how much you can achieve given the amount of time available. For a five- to seven-minute speech, focus on clearly communicating two or three points.

ANALYZING YOUR AUDIENCE

Once you have written down the purpose of your presentation, take a few moments to consider who you will be addressing. Your presentation will vary greatly with your audience. The more you know ahead of time about your audience, the better your chances of being successful and avoiding any surprises. Many experienced speakers make a point to interview several of the members of the audience before a presentation. Your analysis should include finding out who and how many people are going to be in your audience, and what their disposition is.

Build a Composite Audience Member

If you had to describe what most of the audience members have in common, what would you say? What is the average age of the audience? Does the audience include mostly men or women? Does it include upper management, middle management, or hourly employees? How much schooling have audience members had? What is their cultural background? Why will they be at your presentation? What can you generalize about their interests and their knowledge of the topic? These questions are crucial to an effective presentation. Although you

Know Your Audience:
Two Different Audiences Can Have Drastically Different
Reactions to the Same Presentation.

will have a variety of individuals in any group, you
can determine the best way to present your message
by identifying the common traits of the audience.

You might have the same message to communicate to very different groups, but the way you present the message, the points you choose to
emphasize, the type and amount of supporting evi-

dence you use, and the logic you employ should vary according to the group. An important factor in your analysis is the level of knowledge and expertise that the audience has about the topic that you are presenting. You must be several "levels" higher in your familiarity with the topic to have enough credibility for the audience to want to listen to you.

Establish the Probable Disposition of the Group

Are you likely to have a supportive, a hostile, or a neutral group for your presentation? Do they feel strongly toward the topic and have a heavy investment in what you have to say, or are they learning about the topic for the first time? What is their probable disposition toward you? Have they been exposed to you before so that they have a preestablished opinion of your qualifications and expertise? What will they have heard about you? Who will introduce you and what will that person have to say? (Maybe you want to write your own introduction to start your presentation off on the right foot.) What is the reputation of the person who is introducing you, with whom you will be associated? Although it is possible to "take a reading" of the audience during your introduction, you will be limited as to the changes you can make in your presentation at that time. Attempt to predict the attitudes of your audience toward you and the topic beforehand.

The last ingredient in determining the disposition of the group is answering the question "What do they expect?" What have they heard your presentation is about? If they have heard little, you will want to spend more time outlining the purpose of your presentation. If they view your presentation as a "cure-all" for many of their problems, you may have to clearly define the parameters of your discussion and limit their expectations.

Estimate the Size of the Group

How many people are going to be listening to your presentation? If you don't have very many people in your audience, your presentation usually can be more informal, with a greater emphasis on discussion. As the size of the audience becomes larger, your communication is apt to be more one-way and more formal. The size of the audience will affect the type of audiovisual aids you will use, but more importantly, it will help you establish a mental image of the presentation that will be invaluable as you begin to prepare and practice your presentation.

When you give a presentation to a large group, your presentation must be easier to understand. Your points must be fewer and better supported, your visuals simple and easy to comprehend, and your style amplified so that gestures and vocalization are easily understood. With a small group you have many chances to correct and modify your statements; with a large group, the amount of modification you can do during your presentation is limited.

ESTABLISHING THE SETTING

The next step in planning your presentation is to find out about the environment in which you will be speaking. Prior to your presentation you will have a significant amount of control over factors involving your speaking environment. However, you will have this control only if you are foresighted enough to think about the setting in which your presentation will occur. For instance, it will not matter how effective your presentation is if the majority of the audience is upset because they had difficulty finding parking places. However, most problems with the presentation setting can be corrected in advance. Let's consider the purpose, timing, and location of your presentational setting.

Purpose of the Meeting

You have already considered your purpose in communicating information in your presentation, but the purpose of the meeting itself should also be considered. Is the audience being assembled primarily to listen to you, or will you be sharing the platform with other speakers or between other agenda items? If you are the sole attraction of the group's attention, you need to take more responsibility in ensuring that all accommodations are perfect. Otherwise, any problems that audience members experience will more directly reflect on the effectiveness of your presentation.

Another way to determine how important a role you will be playing for the audience is to find out what they will be doing prior to and after your presentation. If you are the last person to speak on a day-long agenda, it is a safe bet that you will have a hard time holding the audience's attention. Or, if you are in the latter third of a two-hour staff meeting, it is likely that you will start later than you had planned, and you will probably have less time than you expected. You might even be asked to simply present your presentation summary!

What is the tone of the occasion? Is it somber and serious, or routine and informal? Is it a one-time presentation aimed at solving a specific problem, or is it a status report for a longstanding committee? The tone or atmosphere of the speaking event should be a factor in the design and delivery of your presentation.

Timing of Your Presentation

Professional presenters are conscious and considerate of time, and you should be too. Specifically determine the time parameters allocated to you. Do not needlessly go overtime or back down on a time commitment given to the group. If you do have an occasional need to go beyond a prearranged time, ask permission of the group. You might poll the group to see if a break is needed. Time your presentations and adjust them accordingly if the sessions run too long or too short. Plan to have a means of tracking the time while you are speaking. If you forget your watch, borrow one or have a member of the audience signal you when time is running low.

Allow enough time to prepare for and to practice (at least five to six times) your presentation. Avoid waiting until the last minute to plan your presentation. Treat preparation and practice of your presentation as a priority. Everyone who gives presentations has other time pressures. You must realize that no performance is polished without adequate time dedicated toward practice.

The final aspect of time that should be considered is the chronological timing of the presentation. An afternoon presentation, right after lunch, had better be very exciting and involving for the audience or most of them will be lost to digestion. Likewise, meetings at the end of the day or just before lunch will have a growing number of audience members watching the clock. Common sense dictates that presentations given on Friday afternoons will have the same timing problems. You might consider the schedule of activities of the organization, such as paydays, holidays, and peak business times during the month. Presentations may be less effective during the yearly budget process of the company if most people are preoccupied with that activity, or during summer months when key decision-makers are on vacation.

Location of Your Presentation

The final element to consider in analyzing the setting for your presentation is its physical location. This can seem basic and mundane, yet if not properly attended to, it can result in disaster for your presentation. For example, will the presentation be inside or outside the work setting? If it is at work, you can plan on a greater number of interruptions, latecomers, and early leavers. More minds will probably be on the business aspects of audience members' jobs than on your presentation. A presentation away from the office is apt to have more of a captive audience, especially if there is limited access to telephones.

Find out how the facilities meet the needs of the audience, the presentation, and yourself. You will probably need some type of audiovisual equipment, which should be set up and tested well in advance of the presentation. If you will be operating the audiovisual equipment, you should check to see that it functions (and how to operate it). Other items might include name tags, markers, coffee, and distribution materials. A complete list of room arrangements will be presented later in this book.

What type of chairs will your audience have? Soft armchairs are desirable if the audience has to sit for any extended length of time. Plastic chairs or straight-backed chairs might be more appropriate if you anticipate problems in holding attention. How will the chairs be arranged? A circular or U-shaped arrangement encourages discussion between audience members if that is desired. Grouping chairs together at tables encourages a team atmosphere, and chairs placed in rows, all facing the speaker, is a standard one-way lecture format.

Is the room carpeted? You might think this a minor detail, but it is very important in promoting a relaxed atmosphere, as well as in saving your feet if you will be standing for very long! Is the lighting adequate for reading? Can it be dimmed if there is a film or slide presentation? Will you have a lectern? Will you have a microphone if needed? Your evaluation of the location and facilities should give you an accurate picture of what it will feel like to give your presentation in that setting. If possible, visit the actual room in which you will be speaking; plan to give at least one practice presentation in the same room.

FIGURING OUT WHAT TO SAY

Now that you have completed your analysis of the purpose, audience, and setting, you should have a much clearer idea of what to communicate. You should have an idea about the audience's beliefs about and attitudes toward the subject, and a very clear understanding of where you want them to be. Remember, your job is to move the audience members from their existing level of awareness on the topic to the new level of awareness that you want them to have!

Step One: Jot Down Your Ideas

Now it is time to write down all your ideas for the presentation. There are two basic questions you can ask yourself that will best show you what information should be included in your presentation.

- What can you tell the audience that they do not already know (or what information do you want them to remember from your presentation)?
- What information would be convincing to the audience (or what would convince you if you were a member of the audience)?

Now, just brainstorm for a minute, and write down all the ideas that come to mind when you answer these questions. Don't let yourself be critical of any of your ideas at the moment. Just let your mind "wander" and write down your ideas; you can throw out the bad ideas later on.

Step Two: Prioritize Your Information

Order the ideas and information you want to present from most important to least important. Your ordered list of ideas and information will enable you to define your purpose in terms of more tangible objectives, and will help you attain those goals. Now you are ready for the next chapter, which will help you to organize all of this information.

4

Preparing Your Presentation

Now that you've completed the planning stage, you are ready to start preparing your presentation. Your presentation will have an introduction, a body, and a conclusion. This chapter teaches you how to write an introduction that will catch everyone's attention, how to structure the body of your presentation to best fit the information you want to present, and how to write a conclusion that reviews the main points of your presentation and leaves the audience right where you want them to be.

It's usually easiest if you first outline the body of your presentation and then develop the introduction and conclusion. This is because the body is the central part of your message, whereas the introduction and conclusion are the trimmings. Often you'll think of clever ideas for your introduction and conclusion while you are preparing the body of the presentation. During the planning stage, you listed

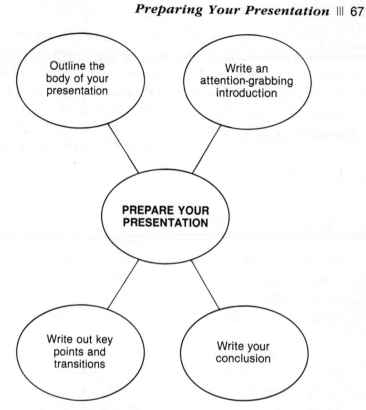

Prepare Your Presentation.

and prioritized the points you want to make during your presentation. Let's now see how you can work this information into the body of your presentation.

PREPARING THE BODY OF YOUR PRESENTATION

The body is the main thrust of a presentation, and most of your delivery time will be spent on the body of your presentation. The body contains the key points you want to convey to the audience, and each point is backed up with convincing supporting data. The first thing you need to do is decide how you want to organize the points you want to make. You need an organizational scheme that best fits your purpose, audience, and personal delivery style. Let's look at some different ways to organize your presentation.

Choosing a Format

There are numerous ways to logically present your information. The format you use should fit your purpose, audience, and style of delivery. Let's look at some formats for organizing your presentation.

Persuasive Formats. Many presenters want to persuade an audience to buy their product or to see things their way. Let's look at some ways to organize your presentation to persuade your audience.

1. *Proposition and Proof.* This form of organization goes back to the famous Greek orator Aristotle. In the prosposition and proof format, you state your idea or position in the beginning of your presentation and then dedicate most of the presentation to justifying or proving that idea or position to the audience. This is a very straightforward method of persuasion that moves the audience logically, step by step, to a conclusion. It is best to use this format when everyone in the audience is familiar with your topic—that way

you can spend your time proving your premise, rather than explaining background information to the uninformed.

2. *Problem-Solution.* The problem-solution format derives from the scientific problem-solving pattern. In this approach you define the problem and then explore possible solutions, citing feasible alternatives. The preferred alternative, or best solution, is saved for last. In this way less desirable alternatives can be considered and rejected, leaving the speaker's proposal as the most desirable. This is an extremely effective format for persuasion, especially when the problem is complicated and the audience is either unfamiliar with the topic or hostile to the proposal. It is also effective as a teaching device, because the audience is led through a systematic development of the topic and alternatives are considered along the way.

3. *Psychological Progression.* This format is similar to the problem-solution format. It also follows a natural decision-making psychology, which makes it a persuasive style to employ. This format, after arousing interest through the introduction, takes the audience through a series of steps by which the speaker seeks to create and then to use a mood of dissatisfaction. As the presentation continues, the speaker clarifies the area of dissatisfaction through the information presented, and finally illustrates the concrete results and benefits that

come from his or her proposal. The psychological progression is similar to the problem-solution format, but it focuses on the individual needs and feelings of the audience members.

Examples of Persuasive Formats. Let's walk through three outlines of presentations on the same topic that use the three different techniques of persuasion: proposition and proof, problem-solution, and psychological progression. Each of these presentations attempts to convince the audience that a particular make of automobile, the Toyorolla, costs the consumer less per year than any other car on the market.

1. *Proposition and Proof.* Remember, in the proposition and proof format you state your premise up front and then spend the rest of the presentation proving it. Below is the outline of the Toyorolla presentation in the proposition and proof format

---

Purpose: Persuade the audience that Toyorollas are the best buy for the money

Premise: Toyorollas give consumers the *most* for their money

A. A study of different cars driven in America in the past five years.
B. The study surveyed three different factors:

- Average purchase price of the automobile
- Average life of the automobile
- Average maintenance cost per year of the automobile

C. Results of the study:

NOTE: Cost/Yr. = Price + Lifetime Maint. ÷ Life.

Auto	Price	Life	Lifetime Maint.	Cost/Yr.
Toyorolla	$14,000	8	$ 8,000	$2,750
Car A	$ 8,000	4	$ 4,000	$3,000
Car B	$25,000	8	$12,000	$4,625

2. *Problem-Solution.* With the problem-solution format, you first define a problem and then explore various solutions to the problem throughout your presentation. Below is the outline of the Toyorolla presentation in the problem-solution format

Purpose: Convince the audience that buying a Toyorolla will reduce their automobile costs

Premise: How can you reduce your automobile costs?

A. Alternative #1: Buy an expensive car
   Main Drawback: Expensive cars tend to

last a long time, but maintenance tends to be more expensive.

Auto	Price	Life	Lifetime Maint.	Cost/Yr.
Car A	$40,000	10	$20,000	$6,000
Car B	$30,000	8	$10,000	$5,000
Car C	$25,000	8	$12,000	$4,625

B. Alternative #2: Buy a cheap car
   Main Drawback: Cheap cars don't last very long, and thus they really aren't so cheap.

Auto	Price	Life	Lifetime Maint.	Cost/Yr.
Car D	$8,000	4	$4,000	$3,000
Car E	$8,000	5	$8,000	$3,200
Car F	$9,000	4	$4,000	$3,250

C. Alternative #3: Buy a medium priced car—in particular, the Toyorolla gives you the most for your money!!

Auto	Price	Life	Lifetime Maint.	Cost/Yr.
Toyorolla	$14,000	8	$8,000	$2,750
Car G	$18,000	6	$6,000	$4,000
Car H	$19,000	7	$7,000	$3,714

3. *Psychological Progression.* In the psychological progression format, you seek to cre-

ate audience/dissatisfaction in the first part of your presentation, and then you illustrate how to reduce or eliminate that dissatisfaction. Here's the Toyorolla presentation using the psychological progression format.

Purpose: Convince the audience that they are wasting money (giving their money away) when they buy other brands of cars. Show them how the Toyorolla is the best buy on the market.

A. The average person spends at least $3,000 every year on an automobile. That's about 10 percent of the national average income, and automobile expenses aren't even tax deductible!

B. Where's all that money going to?
   - Average maintenance cost/year, $1,000
   - Average purchase price, $17,000
   - Average life of automobile, 4 years

C. Will purchasing a cheaper car reduce these costs?
   No. Cheap cars don't last very long and thus they really aren't so cheap.

Auto	Price	Life	Lifetime Maint.	Cost/Yr.
Car D	$8,000	4	$4,000	$3,000
Car E	$8,000	5	$8,000	$3,200
Car F	$9,000	4	$4,000	$3,250

D. Maybe purchasing an expensive car that lasts longer is the solution.

No. Expensive cars tend to last a long time, but maintenance tends to be more expensive.

Auto	Price	Life	Lifetime Maint.	Cost/Yr.
Car A	$40,000	10	$20,000	$6,000
Car B	$30,000	8	$10,000	$5,000
Car C	$25,000	8	$12,000	$4,625

E. How about a medium-priced car?

Yes. There's only one medium-priced car that gives you the most for your money: the Toyorolla!!

Auto	Price	Life	Lifetime Maint.	Cost/Yr.
Toyorolla	$14,000	8	$8,000	$2,750
Car G	$18,000	6	$6,000	$4,000
Car H	$19,000	7	$7,000	$3,714

From these three examples, you can see that the proposition and proof format is a very straightforward method of persuasion. The problem-solution format is a persuasive format that leads the audience to a logical conclusion. The psychological progression format involves the emotions and leads the audience to a logical and emotional conclusion.

Chronological Format. A chronological organization relates a process or series of events in the order in which they occurred. Chronological formats are well suited for presentations that take a historical view of a problem or situation or have a narrative tone throughout.

Cause-and-Effect Format. This organizational format first outlines various causes of a situation and then describes the effects of each. It is useful for examining possible future events. For example, if event A leads to B and B leads to C, what are the chances that event C will occur, and if it does, what can we do about it? This format can be reversed so that effects or results are discussed first and then possible causes are considered. This reverse format is useful for analyzing a present problem.

Compare-and-Contrast Format. This format examines how several things are similar and then how they are different, which is often a valuable process for deciding between alternative actions.

Order-of-Decreasing-Importance Format. This method lists information from most important to least important, and can be especially effective in making sure an important piece of information is not missed by the audience. Attention is usually greatest at the beginning of a presentation. The reverse of this format—the order of increasing importance—is effective in adding a dramatic or suspenseful flair to your presentation.

Simple-to-Complex Format. This organization starts with simpler concepts and builds to more complex and abstract ones. It is effective for teaching, since the speaker begins with what the audience currently knows and gradually introduces more advanced ideas. The reverse organization, sometimes called backward chaining, explains the "big picture" to the audience and then describes the specific subelements of that complicated process. For example, in explaining how a computer works you must first describe the general theory behind computers before you relate a step-by-step description of what happens.

Classification Format. This method of organization involves convenient categories for presenting and remembering information. It is an effective method for breaking up a list of items so that the presentation does not become boring or difficult to follow, as is often the case when a speaker announces he or she will present fourteen reasons for accepting a proposal.

Physical Location Format. This is an effective format for certain types of presentations, such as a descriptive presentation of a new office complex. This method follows a visual pattern for what is being discussed, such as the exterior of the building, the interior, adjacent facilities, and convenience of parking locations. This format can also be used in describing geographical information.

Experiment with Different Formats

Go through the following list of formats and check off which one or ones you think might best fit your purpose, audience and style of delivery.

Proposition and proof   _____
Problem-solution   _____
Psychological progression   _____
Chronological   _____
Cause and effect   _____
Compare and contrast   _____
Order of decreasing importance _____
Simple to complex   _____
Classification   _____
Physical location   _____

Now take some time and write out your main points, using or combining the formats you checked off. Experiment with different formats to discover which one or ones are most effective for your purpose, audience, and style of delivery.

Select Supporting Data

In the previous sections you chose a format or formats and wrote out the main points of your presentation. Now you are ready to back up those points with supporting data. Supporting data serve several purposes in your presentation. The most important purpose they serve is to add credibility to your statements. When data are used appropriately, statements and opinions can take on a factual tone that will make your presentation more convincing.

Supporting information can also be used to clarify a point you are trying to make. When a point is complex or abstract, additional information or data can help an audience to visualize and more easily comprehend your meaning. Since different people learn best in different ways, added examples, data,

Supporting Data Add Credibility to Your Presentation.

or other supporting information will increase the percentage of the audience that comprehends and is convinced by your arguments.

A third reason for using supporting information in a presentation is to make it more interesting. Examples and stories break up the presentation of information and refocus the group's attention. Audience members typically enjoy stories and often will remember them long after other points in your presentation are forgotten.

Following is a discussion of the most common types of supporting data that you can incorporate in your presentation.

Statistics. Statistics are numbers, percentages, dollars, and facts. They can add instant credibility to a statement and make an opinion sound like a fact. Many listeners will always think more of a statement that begins, "A recent study indicated that . . ." The advantage of using statistics in your presentation is the added credibility they give you and your statements. Statistics can be manipulated to your advantage. For example, if your company sold four hundred thousand units of a certain product, representing a three percent increase in units sold from the previous year, you would use the figure of four hundred thousand units if you wanted to create the impression that sales were significant, and the three percent figure if you wanted to make the same sales seem insignificant.

Statistics are most effective when you give the audience a comparison they can relate to easily. For example, a new type of paint may cover six hundred square feet per can, which is not necessarily impressive unless you are also told that a typical can of paint covers only three hundred fifty square feet. The closer the comparison is to the listeners' experience and the more surprising the contrast is to the listener, the more impressive and convincing the information will be. Another way of making statistics stand out is to round off numbers. For example, 5,779 can become "almost six thousand," 332 can become "hundreds," and March through June can become "a quarter of a year."

Examples. Examples are representative cases of an occurrence or an object. They are best at clarifying potentially confusing statements or at bringing vague, general abstractions down to specific, concrete applications. The major disadvantage of examples, if they are used incorrectly, is that by themselves examples cannot prove a point. An example you cite can always be discredited by the audience as being an isolated case.

To make an example more credible, try to indicate why it is typical and representative. To support the contention "Quality assurance in manufacturing is difficult to maintain," do not simply state "I went down to observe the production line twice this week and both times rejection rates were high." Rather, "Two randomly selected days in which production was normal showed high rejection rates, which correlated with industrywide findings concerning quality assurance."

Another way of making examples more effective is to try to use some from your personal experience. This will keep them from sounding academic or contrived, while enhancing the credibility you have with respect to the topic.

Stories. Stories are expanded examples, which also serve to reinforce a specific point. They are almost always welcomed by members of the audience, because people generally enjoy listening to stories. As with examples, the recounting of an event or occurrence can make a point clearer because it is easier to "see" a graphic description than to envision abstract concepts. The disadvantage of stories is that they are difficult to use effectively. Speakers often make the mistake of being long-winded and giving unnecessary details, rambling, or going off on unrelated tangents. At other times, speakers may become redundant or backtrack so that the story becomes boring and the audience becomes anxious for the speaker to get to the point.

Stories are most effective when there is a logical order and movement to what is said. Make sure the story ties in well with the information presented both before it and after. Work on your style by practicing in your everyday conversations the dramatic or suspenseful relaying of experiences. The ability to weave an interesting yarn will always be an asset.

Quotations. Quotations are statements that someone else has made. They add a certain class and formality to your presentation, but, like examples, they do not prove your points. The other disadvantage is that it is not difficult to find an opposing quote for any statement. For that reason quotations should not be relied on as evidence for your presentation, but rather as support for the style and delivery of your communication.

The value of a quote inevitably rests on how well known the originator was or is, and on the audience's level of knowledge concerning the topic under discussion. Sometimes it is best to directly read a quote for the added emphasis it will bring to your presentation. You may use the indicators *quote* and *end quote* when being formal; otherwise, it will suffice to simply lead off with the quote by saying, "One expert states that . . ." or, "In the words of . . ."

Write Your Transitions

Now that you have your main points and your supporting data, it is time to develop how you are going to smoothly make the transition from one main point to the next. Transitions start with the current thought and explain a reason or rationale for moving to the next thought. With good transitions you will keep your audience right with you. Planning out your transitions ahead of time will help you remember the order and flow of your presentation. Transitions can help your presentation in the following ways.

Emphasize Your Organization. Transitions are your opportunity to emphasize what you have covered already and where you are headed. If you are giving a presentation in a chronological format, you might say something like: "So in the last five years our company has been devoted to researching a system that would best meet your needs. Now we have developed the system, and this is our plan for the next five years . . ."

Grab the Audience's Attention. You may have lost the audience during your last point. You can throw an attention-getter into your transition to wake up the audience and get them ready for your next point.

Help You Remember the Flow of Your Presentation. Planning out your transitions links the main points of your presentation and helps you remember what you need to say when you actually deliver your presentation.

WRITING YOUR INTRODUCTION

A good introduction grabs your audience's attention and prepares them for what you have to say. It states the premise of the presentation and indicates why

A Good Introduction Must Grab the Audience's Attention.

the topic is significant. It creates a desire in audience members to know more about what you have to say. Your introduction paves the way for the rest of your presentation.

The importance of a well planned, effective introduction cannot be stressed enough. Although it is not a fair practice, most audience members will make a judgment about you and your presentation based on only the first few minutes of contact. Unfortunately, you will not get a second chance to make your first impression! Even the shortest presentations need a well-planned opening. Without an interested and alert audience, your presentation doesn't stand a chance of being effective.

You need to involve the audience in your presentation by mentally pulling them into the topic, or at times even physically involving them, as in asking for a show of hands or soliciting an overt response. An effective introduction will capture an audience's attention, put everyone at ease, preview what you have to say, and explain why your message is important. Let's examine why and how to best meet these four purposes, and then detail a variety of effective introductions that you might use.

Capture the Audience's Attention

Most audiences are not mentally "with" a speaker when he or she first begins to speak. They are in their own worlds, planning what they will be doing later that day, thinking about a problem they are having, or just plain daydreaming. Initially, audience members observe rather than listen to a speaker. That is, they will first notice your manner, dress, and other nonverbal aspects, and will use those to form an opinion about your credibility. An effective introduction pulls the wandering minds into the room and specifically focuses the attention of the audience on you, the speaker, and your topic.

A few moments of preparation for an effective opening will keep you from charging off and leaving your audience behind. If members of an audience tune in in midsentence to what you are saying, several minutes after you have begun to speak, you can be sure that they will be confused and miss the point of many of the items you are relating. Their attention will revert to the previous mental activity they were engaged in. An attention-getter increases the chance that your audience will be with you as you proceed to the body of your message.

The other key aspect of any effective attention-getter is that it be relevant to the topic of discussion or the immediate speaking situation. There are numerous inappropriate ways to grab the attention of a group of people. For example, many speakers automatically begin presentations with the latest joke they have heard, whether it is relevant to the situation or not. Don't make this same mistake. If you cannot tie your attention-getter in with your topic, choose another opening. Consider how one speaker took a play on words and made it into an effective, appropriate opening. "I called the driving school this morning and they signed me up for a *crash* course. In the next ten minutes I want to *drive* home the point that automobile safety is no accident."

Here are some of the most common methods for opening a presentation and getting the attention of the audience.

Ask a Question. Ask a rhetorical question that needs no answer or one that seeks an overresponse from the audience. Either type involves the audience by getting them to think about the topic. If you do want the audience to respond, make sure it is easy for them to do so. Ask a question that can be answered with a "yes" or "no," or call for a show of hands. Here are some examples:

- How many here have ever been confused about federal tax forms?
- Would you know what to do if the person next to you started choking?
- Who here owns an imported car?

An initial question in your introduction can also be helpful in confirming or gathering information about your audience that may be valuable in tailoring the remainder of your presentation.

State an Impressive Fact.   Begin with an unusual and impressive fact or statistic that supports the theme of your presentation. For example:

- The number of our competitors has doubled in the last five years.
- One person out of every five in this room will die of cancer.
- More people will watch TV tonight than the total number of people that have seen all of the stage performances of all of Shakespeare's plays.

Tell a Joke.   This is a traditional way for a speaker to warm up an audience. Be sure the joke is appropriate. If you have any doubts, select another joke or a different way of beginning. Also be sure that the joke can be made relevant to the topic under discussion or to the speaking situation. Some people are better at using one-liners, while others can be effective with longer, humorous stories. Experiment with each and see what works best for you. It may be safer to start with a joke that you have heard when you were part of another audience and that you particularly liked. Keep track of such jokes in a small notebook and soon you will have an entire library of funnies to adapt to various situations.

Tell a Story.   A personal story relating an experience you have had with some aspect of the topic being discussed is an excellent way to begin a presentation. People are drawn to hearing about the experiences of others, and in the presentational setting such a story will also enhance your credibility. Stories are easy to visualize and are thus effective for communicating information.

Use a Quotation.   Quotations are interesting introductions for presentations. You can always find a quote that will fit your topic and perhaps even the situation. Quotations add to the credibility of your presentation and to your style of delivery.

Make an Emphatic Statement.   A forceful statement is bound to capture the attention of your audience and to set a dynamic tone for the remainder of your presentation. "It's time we stop letting the high cost of quality tools eat up our profits!"

No matter what type of introduction you select, be sure that it is upbeat, positive, and foolproof. It is the part of your presentation that is worth practicing a few times more than other parts of your speech. Here are some other miscellaneous suggestions concerning your introduction that you should consider.

Put the Audience and Yourself at Ease

You need to give your audience a chance—no matter how brief—to get to know you before you can expect them to trust the information you have to communicate. An effective introduction serves to relax both the audience and you. One reason humor is so popular in an introduction is that laughter gives everyone an energy release, which instantly improves the attitude of the listeners. This initial activity in a presentation is often referred to as "warming up the audience." It serves to set a mutually acceptable tone for your presentation and a rate and style of delivery that is acceptable to the audience. A speaker who continues delivering information when he or she senses that the audience is not in tune with the presentation is asking for trouble.

Preview the Topic

To eliminate the possibility of any confusion, the speaker should clearly state the purpose of the presentation. The purpose, as determined in your preliminary analysis, should be stated in terms of what the audience can expect from the forthcoming presentation. For example, you may want to begin this part of your introduction with a phrase such as "Prior to leaving today, each person present should have a better understanding of . . ." or "After hearing this presentation the audience will be able to . . ."

State the Significance of the Topic

Very few topics will automatically be perceived as relevant to the needs of all members of your audience. Even if the benefits of your presentation seem obvious to you, it is a good habit to take a moment to explain why your presentation should be of value to everyone in the audience. Chances are that even those who initially believed your presentation would be of value probably focused on only a single benefit. You can provide several reasons why your presentation will be beneficial.

The significance statement should be worded from the listener's perspective so that it touches members of the audience personally. Say, for example, "This presentation will show you how to save hundreds of dollars on your next car purchase," instead of "This presentation will discuss possible savings when purchasing a car." You want to suggest that the information to be presented will have a real, immediate value for the listener—that the communication is not an academic exercise but has very practical applications.

Not only should you state why the topic is of importance to the audience, but you should also indicate why it is especially timely. What makes your information more important today than it was last year or will be next year? What are the possible consequences if action is not taken soon? These are questions you should consider in building a sense of urgency and, correspondingly, a "freshness" for the topic.

The statement of significance is an excellent way of concluding your introduction because it creates interest. It provides a reason for the audience to continue to give you their attention. Some speakers effectively emphasize the significance of the presentation by concluding the introduction with a question such as: "Is ten minutes of your undivided attention worth the benefits I just described as being possible? If so, listen closely . . . ."

Don't Be Negative

Do not apologize for a lack of preparation or any other inadequacy of your speaking situation. Do not insult or offend your audience. Instead, focus on what is positive about the situation, the group, and what you have to offer them. Be confident in your manner and your word selection. Be enthusiastic about speaking and avoid mundane starts such as "Today I'm going to talk about . . ." or "Mr. So-and-So asked me to give this talk."

Be Concise and Dynamic

An introduction should be brief. It should start strong and pull the audience into the topic of the presentation. Do not ramble or in other ways be long-winded in your opening remarks. Don't buffer your first statement with comments such as "Before I begin my presentation, I would like to take a few minutes to . . ." or "I guess the best way to start is to give you a description of all my previous experience with this type of problem." Either of these are guaranteed to put your audience to sleep, perhaps before you finish the sentence.

WRITING YOUR CONCLUSION

Your conclusion reviews what you have discussed in your presentation in a way that makes the key points of your message memorable to the audience. Most conclusions have some type of call to action, in which the speaker suggests that audience members do or think something different as a result of the information just presented.

Most of what has been said for the introduction applies to the conclusion as well. Your close should be planned exactingly. It should be brief and motivational. The following are some tips for writing your conclusion.

Review Your Main Points

Summarize the points you have made, focusing not so much on what was said as on what should be remembered and why. Repeat the purpose of the speech and its main points, or rephrase this information.

Make a Call to Action

Because most presentations are intended to change the thinking or behavior of the audience, make it clear exactly what each member of the group should do if he or she has been convinced by your presentation.

Tie Back in to the Introduction

Your presentation will appear extremely polished and well planned if you return to your introductory remarks. Add on to a story you began your presentation with by providing a new twist or variation, additional insight or explanation.

Don't Ramble On

Do not continue talking after you have finished your prepared presentation. Don't say "Another thing I meant to mention" or "One more item I wanted to cover is . . . ." If you are at a loss for words as you approach the close, simply repeat your contention and sit down. No new information should ever be presented in your conclusion, especially not if it was something that you simply forgot to mention. No one will be the wiser that you failed to include the information.

Don't Just Stop

You need a smooth closing to your presentation, not an abrupt ending that leaves the audience scratching their heads. Never say "And that's all I have to say," or offer any type of apology such as "I'm sorry I wasn't better prepared, but hope you picked up something."

PREPARING NOTES FOR YOUR PRESENTATION

Now it is time to develop some notes for your presentation. Notes not only will help you to remember exactly what you want to communicate but will give you a greater sense of confidence in your delivery. You can always refer back to your notes during your presentation if you forget what your next point is. Let's look at some pointers for preparing notes for your presentation.

Use an Outline Format

Your notes should be divided into major and minor headings, arranged in the categories just discussed: introduction, body, and conclusion. Use space, capitalization, or underlining to highlight your key points and to indent supporting information.

Be Brief but Specific

Write just enough in your notes to remember the entire thought you wish to convey. Usually this can be key words or statistics you want to be sure to communicate accurately. Do not simply write "story," because you may forget exactly what story you had in mind. Instead, state something unique about the story that is likely to jog your memory, such as "Jones account story" to convey an example you have from a recent interaction with a customer. When you practice with your notes, you will find that each time you present your material your outline will have shorter reminders for each point.

Use Only One Note Card

Almost every five-to-seven-minute presentation can be adequately covered on one side of a five-by-seven-inch index card or legal pad. Writing more notes than this increases the likelihood that you will lose your place, shuffle your notes, or read information to the audience—none of which is acceptable. Your note card should be stiff so there is less chance that you will play with it during your delivery, and possibly distract from your presentation.

Write Large Enough to Read

Your notes will not do you much good if you cannot easily read them during your delivery. Print boldly so that this will not be a problem.

Write Out the Key Parts

Because the exact wording is crucial for certain parts of your presentation, write these parts out: a single sentence for each major point, the exact words you will begin and end your presentation with, and the transitional sentences between major sections of your speech. The transitions should be written out because of a tendency to inadvertently omit them during your delivery.

Make Notes to Yourself on Your Note Card

Indicate, for example, where you plan to use a visual aid. If you are using several visual aids, number them for easy reference. Also make notes in the margin to help you check any delivery mistakes you tend to make, such as "steady eye contact," "pause for emphasis," or "slow down."

Sample Notes for a Presentation

The sample notes shown on page 95 are for an hour-long presentation on job hunting given to a group of about fifty people. The longer presentational length required a few more notes, but even then the notes were contained on the top sheet of an 8½-by-11-inch notepad. The presentational notes are followed by a presentational worksheet.

SAMPLE PRESENTATION NOTES

"THE TRUTH BEHIND JOB HUNTING"

INTRODUCTION

Attention: "How many people here know how to hitchhike?"— hitchhiking analogy

Transition: "Job hunting is a lot like hitchhiking"

Significance:

8 million unemployed in U.S.

Average American changes jobs every 3.6 years (twice as fast as 10 years ago)

Chances are in 1 to 2 years you will be in the job market

Transition: Will you know what to do? Most people don't.

BODY

Problem:

Typical Approach

1. *Secondary sources* (want ads, personnel, agencies)
2. *Impersonal* (form letters not to a specific person)
3. *Limited leads* (disadvantages: waiting/wasting time/rejection felt personally/feeling of starting over/treadmill attitude/behavior slump)

Transition: "It doesn't have to be that way, there is an alternative"

Solution:

Alternative Approach: 3 Ps

1. Primary sources (those whom you would work directly for)
2. Personal contacts (phone, individual letters, follow up)

Continued.

3. *P*lenty of leads (advantages: expanding network of contacts/active and confident/rejection less personal (too busy to care)/better chance of offers)

Transition: "That's the way it works, and it can work for you!"

CONCLUSION

Review: "The three Ps—Primary sources, approached in a Personal way, and Plenty of them!"

Action, Twist to Tie in with Intro: "Use these techniques and you will never need to 'hitchhike' for a job again!"

Questions

PRESENTATION WORKSHEET

INTRODUCTION

Attention-Getting Statement_____

_____

Purpose Statement_____

_____

Significance Statement_____

_____

BODY

Overview of Key Points

1. _____

_____

2. _____

_____

3. _____

_____

SPEECH BODY:

Key Point #1_____

_____

Supporting Evidence_____

_____

Supporting Evidence_____

_____

Transition_____

_____

Key Point #2_____

_____

Continued.

Supporting Evidence_____

_____

Supporting Evidence_____

_____

Transition_____

_____

Key Point #3_____

_____

Supporting Evidence_____

_____

Supporting Evidence_____

_____

Transition_____

_____

CONCLUSION

Review of Key Points

1. _____

_____

2. _____

_____

3. _____

_____

Call to Action_____

_____

5

Selecting and Preparing Visual Aids

Visual aids dominate modern presentations. They can be a powerful factor in a successful presentation, turning a good delivery into a great one. Visual aids can be used in a number of ways to enhance your presentation. Among the most common uses are to add emphasis and clarity to specific points of your presentation, to aid in the organization of your presentation, and to hold the interest of the audience. Visual aids allow you to present information through another channel of communication, the visual channel, and thus increase the probability that your message will be effective. Let's examine some of the advantages and disadvantages of some of the most common visual aids used for presentations today.

CHOOSING YOUR VISUAL AIDS

Often the visual aids you use depend on how much time you have available to prepare them, how much money you can spend to make them, what facilities are available at the location of your presentation and, frequently, what standards your organization has about its audio and visual aids.

Transparencies

Perhaps the most versatile of visual aids are transparencies shown on an overhead projector. Transparencies consist of a clear film on which are drawn images, graphics, and text. They can be used with groups ranging from five to about one hundred people. If you have the time and the budget, transparencies that are made professionally look great! Professionally created transparencies include nice graphics, different colored transparencies, and overlapping sections to accent your presentation.

Advantages Associated with Using Transparencies. Other than the obvious advantages associated with having any type of visual aid in your presentation, transparencies offer some unique advantages.

1. *Transparencies Can Be Generated Quickly.* Transparencies can be generated very quickly using computer graphics. If you have a computer-graphics package, you can design your presentation on a computer, print

out your presentation on a graphics printer, and create the transparencies from the graphics printouts using a copier machine.

2. *Transparencies Provide the Flexibility of a Chalkboard.* Another nice feature of transparencies shown on an overhead projector is that you can use the overhead projector like a chalkboard. You can write on a transparency to illustrate different points as you speak to the audience.

3. *Use of Transparencies Helps Maintain Control over the Audience.* Another advantage of using the overhead projector is that the room can be partially lit and the speaker can still face the audience. Both of these factors will allow you to have greater control over the audience's attention during your presentation.

4. *You Can Use the Frame on the Transparency for Notes.* You can also make notes on the transparency frame to help you remember additional points to be discussed while presenting each transparency.

Dos and Don'ts of Transparencies. Because it is so easy to create transparencies yourself, make sure you use the following guidelines.

1. *Frame Your Transparencies.* If you don't frame your transparencies, you will find yourself fumbling with them when you give your presentation because they have a tendency to

stick together! Take the time to frame them, or slip them into the plastic covers that are available in office supply stores. The plastic covers are nice because they are usually three-hole punched, and hence you can keep your presentation together in a three-ring notebook.

2. *Make Sure the Information Is Readable on the Screen.* Almost any type of information can be conveyed with transparencies, including drawings, notes, photos, and letters, but you need to make sure that the information is readable when it is projected onto a screen. Transparencies are so easy to make that you might be tempted to copy some existing chart or typed text onto a transparency—*don't* fall into this trap! Typed information, even if it is all uppercase, is very difficult to read and should be avoided. A larger-size type, often called speech type, is readable on the transparency. Computer printouts, maps, and complicated graphs also should be avoided because of the difficulty in reading and understanding such information.

3. *Use One Transparency To Convey Two Minutes' Worth of Information.* The average length of time you spend discussing the information on a transparency should be about two minutes.

4. *Make Sure Your Transparencies Are Not Boring!* Too many transparencies containing words only often make for a boring presentation, especially if the audience has to read a

significant amount of information from the transparencies. Simple transparencies can be made more effective by adding arrows, dots, and other artistic trimmings. Colored sheets of transparency film can be taped over your printed message to make it visually more pleasing.

5. *Don't Pile Your Transparencies before the Audience.* If you put all your slides in front of the audience they will spend time wondering when you will get through them. Keep your transparencies out of sight.

6. *Don't Read from Your Transparencies.* It is OK to use your transparencies as a reminder of what you want to say—but don't read from them to the audience.

7. *Make Copies of Your Transparencies for the Audience.* It is nice to give your audience copies of your transparencies in case some people can't see the screen very well or if some want to make notes on them as you go along.

Flip Charts

Also known as a chart-pac, a flip chart consists of a pad of paper on an easel. It has for the most part replaced the chalkboard in modern businesses.

Advantages. One thing you don't have to worry about with flip charts is that something mechanical will go wrong. About the worst that can happen is that you'll run out of paper or your felt

Don't Pile Your Transparencies in Front of the Audience.

pens will go dry, each of which is pretty easy to solve. Flip charts also offer the following unique advantages:

1. *Great for Making Spontaneous Notes.* The flip chart is excellent for making notes spontaneously while presenting to a group of from five to fifty people, because those notes can then be posted or saved and later typed. I often use flip charts in addition to transparencies to keep notes or explain various points during a presentation.

2. *Great for Training.* The flip chart is great when you are training or consulting with a group—or when you are running a business meeting. Flip charts are very useful for those situations where you are gathering informa-

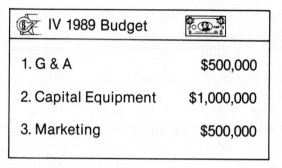

A Good Transparency Design Has
- Nice Graphics
- Large Type
- Simplified Information
- Numbered Points

tion and developing ideas during the presentation. Let's say, for example, you are consulting with a business on strategic planning. You would know the basic process to go through, but you will probably want to use flip charts to track the information and ideas developed with the group.

3. *Flip Charts Can Be Prepared in Advance.* Flip charts can also be prepared in advance and flipped as needed during your presentation. This technique allows for more carefully drawn visuals and a chance to redo mistakes. If you prepare your flip charts in advance, you can pencil in notes to yourself that are not noticeable to the audience.

Dos and Don'ts of Flip Charts. Here are some things to keep in mind when you are creating your flip charts.

1. *Keep Your Writing Legible.* Take the time to write legibly. Try and keep your letters the same height. Make sure you use lined paper—this will help you to letter neatly.

2. *Use Colors for Emphasis.* Colored markers will make your flip charts attention-grabbers, especially if you attempt to represent visually the points you are making verbally.

3. *Use Graphics for Emphasis.* You don't need to be a great artist; just use simple graphics like lines, circles, and squares. Graphics will add variety to your flip charts.

4. *Keep Your Points Brief.* Like any visual aid, don't overload the flip chart with too much information!

35mm Slides

Slide shows can give a presentation the ultimate professional look. Slides are relatively inexpensive to make, but skill is required in designing and producing an effective show, which can be more expensive. Slide presentations are most typically reserved for large, formal meetings of several hundred people or more.

Advantages. No doubt about it, the overriding advantage of using 35mm slides is that your presentation will come off as very professional! For a formal presentation you might have to spend extra time and money preparing the slides, but it will be worth it!

Dos and Don'ts of 35mm Slides

1. *You Have To Work Extra Hard To Keep the Audience Awake.*   Remember, the lights will be out when you deliver a 35mm presentation, and the audience won't be watching you, they will be watching the slides. You have to make sure your presentation is interesting enough to keep the audience with you. Make sure you incorporate a lot of attention-grabbers.

2. *Use Color and Graphics.*   You've gone to the trouble to create 35mm slides for your presentation, so make sure they are colorful with lots of graphics—it'll help keep the audience with you.

3. *Use One Slide To Convey Two Minutes' Worth of Information.*   The average length of time you spend discussing the information on a slide should be about two minutes.

4. *Make and Illustrate Your Points Very Clearly.*   You lose some of your flexibility when you give a 35mm slide presentation (you can't go make a point on a blackboard very easily), so make sure your presentation doesn't have any holes in it!

DESIGNING VISUAL AIDS

Let's look at some rules of thumb for making the most effective visual aids.

Essential

The most important factor in considering any aid is whether it is essential to your presentation. Each aid should present or clarify information vital to your message. There should be no extra visuals just because additional information is available. You should select your aids according to what information will be more easily understood by an audience if it is seen rather than heard. For example, instead of reading a list of supporting data and concluding with more numbers, a visual aid with bar graphs might show a trend more quickly and more easily.

Keep Them Simple

Keep what you communicate visually as simple as possible. For an overhead transparency, for example, use only three to four lines of information per slide; each line should consist only of key words and not entire sentences. Use block lettering instead of fancier type styles. Summarize information; avoid presenting a paragraph or page of data. Have each aid focus only on a single idea and emphasize information that is better seen than heard.

Use Large Print

Regardless of the type of aid you use, it will be useless if it cannot be read by the audience. Check the legibility range yourself by setting up the aid in the room you will be using; then try to read the aid from different areas of the room. For example, when using a flip chart you should write larger.

Label Them

Each aid should be able to stand free of others, or from your spoken words, and still be easily understood. This will increase the chances that your audience will quickly see what the aid is all about, even if they have mentally tuned you out for a few moments. Each aid should be titled or headed so that it is self-sufficient, even if the aid consists only of spontaneous remarks. In that case, use the topic discussion or the question being answered as a heading.

Keep Them Interesting

Use colors, cartoons, pictures, symbols, and drawings to make your aids more interesting and easier to remember. Highlight memory aids for your visuals, such as having the first letter of each key word you wish to discuss spell an easy-to-remember word. Even with these attention-getting additions, your visual should be uncluttered and the additions should not distract from the main points of your presentation.

Number Your Points

Number your key points. Tell the audience up front how many key points you will be discussing. This will help the audience stay with you during your presentation. It also helps them to know how far along you are in your presentation.

USING VISUAL AIDS

Even the best aids can destroy a presentation if they are improperly used. The most important thing to remember is that your visual aids should *support* your presentation, not *be* your presentation. Avoid bringing in a stack of overhead slides and speaking only from those slides. Instead, you should always be the center of attention in your presentation. Always practice with your aid first. What may appear to make sense when you glance at it may be very difficult to explain while standing in front of a group. Here are other tips to observe:

Have Everything in Place

Have your audio and visual aids ready to go prior to the presentation. For transparencies, this may mean having the first one properly centered and focused on the overhead, with the rest in a neat stack nearby. Post flip charts or other prepared visuals in an appropriate position in the front of the room and cover them until it is time for your presentation. Remove all aids from previous presentations before you begin.

Don't Show Them Until You're Ready

As soon as a visual is exposed, it attracts the attention of the audience. If you are still introducing the topic or the visual, chances are great that your spoken words will be missed. When using an overhead projector, you can easily control attention by turning the light on and off. On individual transparencies you can cover specific points on a list by sliding a sheet of typing paper between the slide and the machine—then expose your points as you are ready.

Avoid Holding Up Visual Aids

Although this may be effective when you first show your aid, chances are you will move while speaking and the aid will become distracting. Either post the visual or have someone else hold it while you are speaking.

Speak to the Audience, Not to the Visual Aid

Always face the audience while you are speaking. For effective speaking while using a visual, *point* to the specific area of the visual to which you are referring, *turn* to the audience, and then *speak*. Although this may add several moments to your presentation, it will make your points more clearly understood.

Speak Louder When Using Visual Aids

Because your attention is distracted and the room may be darkened, and because some visual aid machines are noisy, you should increase your vocal level while using aids.

Speak to the Audience, Not to the Visual Aid.

Don't Block the View

Be careful that you, your podium, or other objects do not interfere with any audience member's view of a visual aid. Especially watch the view from the front sides of the audience. This may take some coordinating if you are using several aids, so plan to make time before your presentation.

Use a Pointer

A pointer stick or an extendable pen will make your presentation more professional and what you are pointing out easier to detect. With overhead projectors a pen or arrow may be left stationary on the machine. A pointer helps you to get out of the way of your visual.

Remove Your Visual Aids When Finished

After your point is complete and when your presentation is done, remove your visuals from the audience's view. Again, this will help you to control the attention of the audience; it is also a presentational courtesy on completion of your talk. However, do not pack up your visuals prior to finishing your presentation. This is distracting for audience members and indicates that what you are saying as you mechanically clean up is less important.

USING HANDOUTS

In an informational presentation, handouts can be an effective means of increasing the learning and retention levels of your audience. You must give careful thought to the preparation and use of handouts for a presentation. If you do not, your handouts might end up disrupting your presentation. Here are several guidelines to follow when using handouts.

Distribute Handouts after Your Presentation

If handouts are distributed prior to or during your presentation, audience members will promptly read the material and fade in and out of listening to you. Your message will become very choppy. Instead, build interest for the material you will distribute at the end of your presentation. The fact that you will be handing out materials can also be used to ask audience members not to take notes and to concentrate instead on the speakers. "I see several people taking notes—all of this is summarized in the materials you will each receive, so you might prefer to simply listen for now." The material is more likely to be used later by audience members if you briefly summarize what it contains when it is distributed at the close of the session.

Keep Handout Material Brief

If you want the material to be read, limit it to two or three pages. If you are using only a page or so from a report, copy only that material and indicate what it was excerpted from.

Make all Handouts Self-Explanatory

Use headings, interpretative remarks, keys, and any other necessary information so the material will be fully understandable by audience members at a later date.

Make Sure Handouts Contribute to Your Objective

Too often speakers present handout material that was designed for some other purpose. This often makes your presentation less professional and seemingly thrown together. Like the visual aids, each handout should be essential for clear communication.

With a minimum amount of preparation and skill in using them, visual aids and handouts can enhance your effectiveness. Many companies have specific departments to help with the design and preparation of these visual aids. Use this professional resource if it is available, since it can help broaden the type and number of ideas you have for supporting your message.

VISUAL AIDS CHECKLIST

Here are the guidelines for designing your visual aids. For each visual aid, ask yourself the following questions:

Is it essential?	_____	Is it labeled?	_____
Is it simple?	_____	Is it interesting	_____
Is it large?	_____	Are key points numbered?	_____

Use the following guidelines when you practice your presentation with your visual aids. After you have gone through your practice session, ask yourself the following questions (or have a friend in the audience answer them for you):

Did I have everything in place
   at the start of the presentation?   _____
Did I show any visual aid before
   I was ready?   _____
Did I hold up any visual aids?   _____

Did I speak to the audience, and
  not to the visual aid?   _____
Did I speak loudly enough?   _____
Did I block the view of the audience?   _____
Did I use a pointer?   _____
Did I remove the visual aid when I
  was finished?   _____

6

Practice Makes You Perfect

Once you have finished your preparation you should plan on practicing a minimum of five or six times. The more you practice, the more familiar you'll become with your outline. Like any skill, the more you practice the activity, the better you get. When you practice your presentation, make sure you concentrate on recalling your ideas and their flow—do not spend time practicing the specific wording of your presentation. In other words, do not memorize your presentation! Nobody wants to listen to a presentation that has been memorized. Memorized presentations are stiff, boring, and lack spontaneity. The audience loses confidence in a speaker who has memorized his or her presentation!

This chapter presents some guidelines and a step-by-step method for practicing your presentation.

GUIDELINES FOR PRACTICING

There are a variety of ways to practice your presentation. At the very minimum, you can practice your presentation by going over the outline in your head. Or, for the most effective results, you can practice your presentation in front of a practice group, from your final notes and outline, using your actual audio or visual aids, in the room where your presentation will be conducted. Again, for the most effective results you should use the same room setup and wear the same clothes you plan to wear on the day of your presentation.

Practicing your presentation ahead of time will help you in a variety of ways when you deliver your presentation. Practicing your presentation:

- helps you deliver a smooth flow of information to your audience;
- helps you visualize, anticipate, and feel comfortable the day of your actual presentation;
- helps you visualize and anticipate questions or objections that the audience might have. Practicing your presentation helps you to see things as the audience is going to see them.
- helps you collect a variety of ways to say the same thing. Each time you practice your presentation you may describe your main points slightly differently. In some cases the new way will be an improvement. In other cases the new way will just be a different way. Having a variety of ways to say the same thing reduces the chance that you will forget what you want to

say, and it also helps you to adapt to different audiences.

Let's look at some guidelines for practicing your presentation.

Make Each Practice One Step Closer to the Presentation

Each time you practice your presentation, make your practice session a little more like the real presentation. What this means is that you need to plan your practices. First, you need to look at how much time you have to practice your presentation. Next, you need to map out different practice sessions for your presentation. For example, if you decide that you have time for three practice sessions, your first practice might simply be thinking through the presentation in your head. Then for your next practice session you might stand up in a room and have someone videotape you while you deliver your presentation. Finally, for your third practice session, you might practice in front of a group of your friends in the same room where you will be delivering your presentation.

Moving a step closer to the real thing will give you a sense of approaching your final goal, and you won't feel like you are just rehearsing the same things over and over again. The closer you make your mock presentations to the real presentation, the less inhibited you will be in the actual situation. When you finally present your material, it will seem as if you have already given the presentation several times.

Finish Each Practice Presentation

Don't fall into the trap of starting your presentation over each time you stumble with your words while you are practicing. If you do this, you will find when you deliver your presentation that some parts of it are very familiar to you—and others are not. You will probably have a strong, well-rehearsed introduction and a weak closing. Your closing is just as important as your introduction—give them equal attention!

Try to continue on to the end of your presentation even if you fumble. Simply make a check mark on your outline to indicate where your rough spots are. When you have finished your practice session, go back to those areas that you checked off and rehearse them until you are comfortable with what you want to say. When you've smoothed over the rough spots, run through the entire presentation one more time. This technique will result in a more even presentation. By going through your presentation completely several times, you gain the experience of explaining your points in several different ways.

Time Your Practice Presentations

After the first one or two practice deliveries, time the next few. This will make you more sensitive to your time limits and the pace of your delivery. Try to speak at the same rate as when actually giving the presentation. Most people tend to speak faster during the real delivery than during their practice presentations. Make a note of how your practice presentations compare in length to your real presentation, so that you can adjust accordingly for your next presentation.

Strive for a Conversational Tone

Conversation is easier to listen to and usually more interesting than deliveries that sound too prepared. People usually speak more directly and with more animation in conversation than when delivering a

Time Your Practice Presentations!

presentation to a group. Take note of yourself when you are talking to a friend; note your gestures and your methods for explaining topics. Try to use some of these techniques during your presentation.

When you are practicing, imagine yourself speaking to a friend about the same topic. If you have trouble with making your delivery conversational, invite a friend to your practice and give your presentation to that person. Try making your delivery a typical conversation. All your practices should be in the first person, not in the third person.

Envision the Audience's Response

Particularly in your last few rehearsals, try to imagine how your audience is going to react to your presentation. Examine your analysis of the audience that you developed during the planning stage, and try to predict questions that the audience is likely to have. If you think of a question or objection that might detract from the persuasiveness of your presentation, build that objection or information into your presentation. For example, you might say something like: "Some of you might be asking yourselves, If this is such a great idea, why haven't we done it already? Let me tell you why." You can turn an audience around by incorporating their doubts and objections into your presentation!

Make it a goal of your practice sessions to identify *ten* of the most likely questions or objections you will get during your presentation. If you can't come up with ten questions or objections, you are probably not anticipating all the possible audience

reactions to your presentation. It's better to anticipate questions that do not arise than to wish you had
anticipated a question you cannot answer. In some
companies the only advice passed down from senior
management to new presenters is "Make sure you
can answer any question you might get." You will
win over your audience if you have anticipated their
objections or questions.

Pay Attention to Details and Get Feedback

Perfect practice makes perfect delivery. As you become more familiar with your material and more
confident about your delivery, look for ways to improve. Ask anyone who listens to your practice
deliveries to recommend ways for you to improve.
Use the evaluation form at the end of this chapter
and have someone give you feedback on your
presentation!

After you know your material and feel confident
about your delivery, use a practice session just to
look for ways to polish your presentation. Let's now
look at a three-step methodology for delivering a
polished presentation.

STEP ONE: WARMING UP

Imagine that practicing your presentation is really
like writing a book. Each time you complete a practice session it's as if you have completed another
draft of your book. Your first practice drafts should
simply focus on getting through the material com-

fortably in a steady flow. Here are three progressive steps you can take to make your initial practice sessions as easy as possible.

Prepare Your Mental Draft

There are two different ways of preparing the mental draft of your presentation: running through your presentation in your head or writing it down on paper. You can choose either method, or perhaps you want to try both.

One of the simplest and most nonthreatening ways to review your presentation is to think it through in your head. Get in a comfortable position, perhaps in an easy chair or lying down in bed. Close your eyes and think through your presentation. Imagine the actual words you will use as you give your delivery. Refer to your notes as often as you need to. Concentrate on your transitions, on how one idea leads into another.

If this is a difficult task, you can skip it and attempt another type of practice. For some people a smooth flow of information comes more readily when they write down what they want to say. This *does not* mean you should *memorize* your presentation. Remember, you want to have a variety of methods "in your hip pocket" for describing various points in your presentation. Writing down what you want to say should provide only one way of wording your information for the first practice. Each time you practice you will improve the way your information is presented and increase the number of ways that your ideas and message can be described.

Prepare Your Speaking Draft

After you have mentally run through your presentation, try going over the presentation verbally. Continue to strive for a nonthreatening practice: remain seated and just talk out loud as you go down your outline. Remember to keep what you are saying in the first person; for example, say "It's an important problem we have to discuss today, one that affects each and every one of us," rather than "Then I'll tell them about how important the problem is . . ." Your goal is to use the actual words, or an approximation thereof, that will be used in your presentation.

Prepare Your Standing Draft

After a couple of times through your talking draft, attempt the same practice technique, but standing up. Make a mock podium if you will eventually have one for your final presentation, and begin to fill in the behavior portion of your message—that is, your gestures, eye contact, and other types of nonverbal behavior. In the same way that you are not memorizing words, do not memorize gestures. Specifically practiced gestures almost always come across as staged and artificial. Instead, try a variety of gestures that are natural to you. It is more important for you to become comfortable with the physical space around you and your ability to gesture in general than to try to mimic any specific gesture. Do this by overgesturing, that is, by amplifying your gestures and trying new ones. Wave your arms, point, stretch, pound your fist, grip your hands. Experiment to see what you find effective for your style. At first all the gestures might seem contrived, but with practice and less inhibition, natural gesturing will spring forth from your style.

STEP TWO: GETTING FEEDBACK

After you have warmed up by thinking and talking through your outline a number of times, you should try one or more types of practice drafts to obtain feedback for improvement. Here are several to choose from. You might even try all three for maximum insight into possible improvements.

Mirrored Draft

One of the easiest ways to get additional information about your delivery style is by practicing in front of a mirror. For many speakers this is a simple and effective method of seeing how you come across to an audience. Others find such a practice embarrassing. Try it for yourself and make your own judgment regarding its value in helping your presentation.

Taped Draft

A more effective method of providing feedback is to tape your presentation on audiocassette. First speak in a relaxed position, such as sitting at a desk, and then more formally, while standing. Try to listen to the tape objectively. First, listen for the major areas of the presentation: the introduction, body, and close. Are they all there? Do they flow together smoothly? Do your key points stand out? Is the message persuasive? Once you are satisfied with those basic elements of your presentation, listen a bit more critically and try to answer some of these questions:

- Did you have any verbal faults? Grammar? Pronunciation? "Ahs" and "ums?"
- Were your supporting data clear and convincing?
- Was your tone energetic and your enthusiasm for the topic apparent?
- Did you vary your rate of speech or the pitch of your voice?
- Did you make an effective use of silence?
- Were you within the time limit?

Do not be too critical of your presentation. Be sure to compliment yourself on the strengths of your presentation. If it is available, a videotape of your presentation will provide even more feedback for improvement. Your nonverbal behavior—gestures, facial expressions, and body movements—can be analyzed using a videotape. Have another person critique either the audiotape or the videotape. The added perspective will help you.

Live Audience Draft

Perhaps the best practice for your presentation is to practice on other people. Having an informal audience, no matter what its size or composition, brings you one step closer to the reality of your speaking situation. First attempt your presentation with a member of your household, then someone from your work environment, and ultimately one or more individuals who will actually be a part of your real audience on the day of your presentation.

Besides getting critiques from your audience members, you will have the immediate feedback that comes from reading faces as you speak. When do they look puzzled? When are they smiling or laughing? Do any heads nod in agreement or shake in disagreement? Before your practice session, ask your audience members to watch specific areas in which you want feedback, or ask them pointed questions about your delivery when you are finished: Was I clear throughout? What was the vaguest area? Which points were most convincing and why? Did I convince you of my objective? If not, what more would you need to be convinced? Remember, the audience members should be encouraged to ask you questions during or after your practice presentation. What better way to anticipate the actual questions you are likely to receive?

STEP THREE: MASTERING YOUR ACT

To put the finishing touches on your practice, you should prepare and conduct a dress rehearsal of your presentation. The following are some ideas for polishing your presentation.

Practice the Rough Spots

After you have been through your presentation several times, you may want to practice just the rough spots. Try practicing those areas, along with your opening and closing remarks, key points, and transitions, until they are extremely comfortable. These areas of your presentation can be practiced during spare moments such as when you are in the shower or driving somewhere.

Practice with Revised Notes

As you put your outline to the test in practice you will probably make changes, deletions, and additions to your presentation. If your original note card becomes too cluttered with changes, you may want to rewrite it. If you do, always be sure to make a practice run using the new outline, or you may have trouble with it in your final presentation.

Use Your Actual Presentation Aids

The last practice drafts of your presentation should make use of whatever audiovisual aids or handouts you plan on using during your presentation. Talk through each aid. This will serve as the final check to see if you have too many aids or if any are confusing.

Do a Dress Rehearsal

As if for a play, plan to have a dress rehearsal for your final presentation. Schedule it for the same time of day in the same room as the actual presentation. Wear the clothes you plan to have on for your presentation. Try to have at least a few members of the audience present. Give your presentation without stopping and handle any questions from the individuals there. This activity should erase any lingering doubts you might have concerning your readiness. You really can't do anything better to prepare yourself for your presentation.

COMMONLY ASKED QUESTIONS

Maybe you really hadn't thought about practicing your presentation. Or maybe you had planned to practice your presentation only once. Let's look at some questions you may have been asking yourself while reading this chapter.

1. *Isn't This a Lot of Practicing for a Single Presentation?* You're right—it is a lot of practice. The amount of time that you spend practicing should vary with how difficult the assignment is for you. If you know the topic well and have presented it to the group before, and you are a fairly confident speaker, many if not most of these practice steps can be skipped. These are solely options, of varying degrees of difficulty, for you to choose from. Adapt them to your own style and

schedule as needed. Keep in mind, however, that some experts suggest the amount of time you practice should equal five times the length of your presentation. And, if you are prone to stage fright, up to 75 percent or more of your anxiety can be eliminated with adequate preparation.

2. *Can I Practice Too Much?* Again, you are right—you can. If, the more you practice, the more the same wording comes from your mouth, you are probably overdoing it. You do not want to destroy any freshness or spontaneity in your delivery. Ideally, you want to be comfortable explaining your points in a number of different ways, as you would if you were describing a picture. Only your introduction, transitions, and closing should be closer to a verbatim speech—but stay flexible.

3. *What If I Don't Have Time to Practice My Presentation?* If this is the case, join the majority of speakers. We all have time constraints, but if the benefits of giving a professional presentation are important enough to you, perhaps some of your priorities can be rearranged to allow adequate preparation time. Some speakers keep in mind the rule of thumb that you should have at least 50 percent of your preparation completed at the time you accept any speaking engagement.

If you have no choice about accepting a speaking engagement, you might try some other techniques for keeping your preparation on target. For example, try blocking out time on your schedule specifically to prepare for your presentation, just as you would do for a meeting. Establish deadlines for the different stages of your preparation, with an adequate time buffer should you fall behind. Finally, gain some reassurance from knowing that each presentation will be that much easier and, although there are very few steps in the process that should be omitted, you can try spending less time on each stage as your speaking expertise increases.

PRESENTATION PREPARATION AND PRACTICE SCHEDULE

Use this form to set up your schedule for preparing and practicing your presentation. Mark down the dates on your calendar and plan to stick to them!

Task	Completion Date

1. PLAN MY PRESENTATION

    a. Write out the purpose of my presentation   _____

    b. Learn who my audience is going to be   _____

    c. Find out about the setting   _____

    d. Jot down and prioritize my ideas   _____

2. PREPARE MY PRESENTATION

    a. Outline the body of my presentation   _____

    b. Develop my supporting data for the presentation   _____

    c. Write the transitions between the main points of my presentation   _____

    d. Develop my introduction   _____

    e. Develop my conclusion   _____

    f. Prepare the notes for my presentation   _____

3. DEVELOP VISUAL AIDS

    a. Complete rough drafts of visual aids   _____

    b. Complete finished versions of visual aids   _____

4. PRACTICE MY PRESENTATION

    a. Mental draft   _____

    b. Speaking draft   _____

    c. Standing draft   _____

Continued.

    d. Mirrored draft   _____

    e. Taped draft   _____

    f. Live audience draft   _____

    g. Practice the rough spots   _____

    h. Practice with revised notes   _____

    i. Practice with visual aids   _____

    j. Dress rehearsal   _____

DETAILED PRESENTATION EVALUATION FORM

Give this form to members of your audience when you practice your presentation. Part I includes a form for an overall evaluation of your speech. Parts II through VI include forms for evaluating different aspects of your presentation.

Presenter_____ Date_____

Presentation Title_____

Audience_____ Location_____

Purpose_____

_____

I. OVERALL EVALUATION
    Did the speaker achieve the intended purpose? Why or why not?

    _____

    _____

    EFFECTIVENESS (circle one) 1 = poor 5 = excellent

Presentation	1	2	3	4	5	n/a
Speaker	1	2	3	4	5	n/a
Content	1	2	3	4	5	n/a

II. PRESENTATION CONTENT
    In the lefthand column are listed different aspects of your presentation. Have the audience check off the phrases from the righthand column that best describe those aspects.

1. INTRODUCTION
    (a) Attention-   Too brief   _____
        Getter   Not attention-getting   _____
                       Inappropriate   _____
                       Commanded my attention   _____
    (b) Thesis   Missing   _____
                       Incomplete   _____

Continued.

		Unclear	_____
		Clear and complete	_____
(c)	Significance Statement	Missing	_____
		Too short	_____
		Too long	_____
		Correct	_____
(d)	Overview	Missing	_____
		Too short	_____
		Too long	_____
		Points not numbered	_____
		Correct	_____
(e)	Transition	Missing	_____
		Too short	_____
		Too long	_____
		Correct	_____

2. BODY

(a)	Main Points	Missing	_____
		Unclear	_____
		Too few	_____
		Too many	_____
		Appropriate	_____
(b)	Organization	Missing	_____
		Unclear	_____
		Rambling	_____
		Clear	_____
		Logical	_____
		Effective	_____
(c)	Supporting Data	Missing	_____
		Scant	_____
		Ineffective	_____
		Adequate	_____

Continued.

	Varied	_____
	Effective	_____
(d) Visuals	Ineffective	_____
	Too many	_____
	Poorly designed	_____
	Too few	_____
	Effective	_____
(e) Transitions	Missing	_____
	Too short	_____
	Too long	_____
	Correct	_____

3. CONCLUSION

(a) Summary	Missing	_____
	Too brief	_____
	Too long	_____
	New information	_____
	Effective	_____
(b) Review	Missing	_____
	Ineffective	_____
	Points not numbered	_____
	Memorable	_____
(c) Action	Missing	_____
	Unclear	_____
	Excessive	_____
	Attainable	_____
	Motivating	_____
(d) Closing Statement	Weak	_____
	Ineffective	_____
	Unplanned	_____
	Clear	_____
	Effective	_____
	Strong	_____

Continued.

(e) Fielding	Unprepared	_____
Questions	Rejects questions	_____
	Too abrupt	_____
	Vague	_____
	Rambling	_____
	Effective	_____

III. VERBAL DELIVERY
1. PERSONAL QUALITIES

(a) Enthusiasm	Missing	_____
	Weak	_____
	Unenergetic	_____
	Exciting	_____
	Contagious	_____
(b) Empathy	Missing	_____
	Uncaring	_____
	Aloof	_____
	Sympathetic	_____
	Sincere	_____
(c) Personality	Doesn't show	_____
	Stiff	_____
	Too formal	_____
	Personable	_____
	Likeable	_____

2. VOCAL QUALITIES

(a) Volume	Too low (can't hear)	_____
	Too loud	_____
	No variety	_____
	Correct	_____
(b) Rate	Too slow	_____
	Too fast	_____
	No variety	_____
	Good	_____

Continued.

(c) Pitch   Too high   _____

                   No variety   _____

                   Monotonous   _____

                   Varied and correct _____

(d) Word Selection Inappropriate   _____

                   Poor   _____

                   Heavy jargon   _____

                   Good   _____

                   Effective   _____

(e) Pronunciation Poor   _____

                   Highlights mistakes _____

                   Correct   _____

(f) Enunciation   Mumbles   _____

                   Sloppy   _____

                   Closemouthed   _____

                   Openmouthed   _____

                   Clear   _____

                   Precise   _____

(g) Tone   Abrasive   _____

                   Hurried   _____

                   Choppy   _____

                   Soothing   _____

                   Effective   _____

(h) Flaws   Excessive   _____

                   Annoying   _____

                   Emphasized   _____

                   Minimal   _____

                   Well handled   _____

                   Unnoticed   _____

3. TIME

(a) Delivery Time Too long   _____

                   Too short   _____

                   Right on time   _____

Continued.

IV. NONVERBAL DELIVERY

1. Dress	Inappropriate	_____
	Too casual	_____
	Too formal	_____
	Appropriate	_____
2. Smile	Missing	_____
	Nervous	_____
	Present	_____
	Natural	_____
3. Eye Contact	Scant	_____
	Fleeting	_____
	Limited	_____
	Appropriate	_____
	Extensive	_____
4. Posture	Poor	_____
	Sloppy	_____
	Rigid	_____
	Shifting	_____
	Excessive movement	_____
	Erect	_____
5. Gestures	Missing	_____
	Limited	_____
	Forced	_____
	Natural	_____
	Appropriate	_____
	Dynamic	_____
6. Mannerisms	Excessive	_____
	Uncontrolled	_____
	Limited	_____
	Unnoticed	_____

Continued.

V. COMMUNICATIVE TECHNIQUES

1. Audience
   Involvement

   Over their heads _____

   Marginally interested _____

   Involved _____

   Excited _____

2. Clarity

   Confusing _____

   Vague and rambling _____

   Numbered points _____

   Clear organization _____

3. Humor

   Inappropriate _____

   Excessive _____

   Ineffective _____

   Appropriate _____

   Effective _____

4. Logical
   Appeal

   Poor arguments _____

   Too few arguments _____

   Good arguments _____

5. Psychological
   Appeal

   Focused on needs of speaker _____

   Focused on needs of some
   audience members _____

   Focused on needs of all
   audience members _____

6. Personal
   Appeal

   Nervous _____

   Evasive _____

   Authoritarian _____

   Aloof _____

   Defensive _____

   Confused _____

   Trustworthy _____

   Confident _____

Continued.

	Positive	_____
	Persuasive	_____
7. Emotional	Inappropriate	_____
Appeal	Unmotivating	_____
	Dynamic	_____
	Persuasive	_____

PLEASE WRITE ANY ADDITIONAL COMMENTS BELOW

_____

_____

_____

_____

7

Polishing Your Presentation

Let's look now at some ways that you can go that extra mile and really polish your presentation. Read this chapter; make a list of some of the techniques in this chapter that you want to work on, and then run through another practice of your presentation.

This chapter examines some techniques for making your presentation really effective. We'll first look at some techniques for improving your verbal and nonverbal communication with the audience. Next you will find some guidelines for using humor in your presentation and some rules of thumb for handling questions. Finally you will find some techniques for ending your presentation on the right note.

COMMUNICATING CLEARLY

The following are a few tips for making sure your message is clear and memorable.

Communicate with Pictures and Analogies

You will be easier to listen to and more interesting if you communicate your information with verbal descriptions or pictures, especially if your ideas are abstract. Use examples or stories to illustrate your points. Make sure you use analogies if your presentation includes facts and figures. For example, if your company's profits rose by 2½ percent, explain this figure to the audience in more tangible (and interesting) terms: "Profits are up over $50,000, or the equivalent of one new color TV per employee."

Number Your Points

Number your points for the audience as well as in your notes. This is especially important for the key items you want the audience to remember. Numbering points gives the audience a simple count of how many things they really have to remember and follow. It helps the audience map out where they are in your presentation and how much farther they have to go. Numbering your points also gives you the added benefit of appearing organized and well prepared.

Emphasize Your Organization

Let your audience know frequently where you are in your presentation and where you are headed. Repeat your organization and key points to help the audience remember your main ideas. If your main points are organized in a way that is logical or catchy, stress that organization even more. "I want us to **STOP** what we are doing. That is, to Structure the Organization's Priorities before additional resources are wasted. I think we should **STOP** now, and I'll tell you why." In this case, an acronym helps to clarify the organization.

YOUR VERBAL AND NONVERBAL DELIVERY

When you are giving your presentation people will be listening to what you say as well as how you say it. They will be trying to read between the lines. Your verbal and nonverbal qualities contribute to your message. Let's look at some different aspects of verbal and nonverbal communication.

Verbal Communication

Your words and how you say them constitute your verbal communication to the audience. Here are some tips for achieving good verbal communication during your presentation.

Show Enthusiasm. One of the most valuable traits you can show your audience is enthusiasm for the topic you are discussing. Enthusiasm will make up for a number of other deficiencies you might have in your presentation. Your enthusiasm for your topic, the situation, and the audience helps create interest in what you have to say and motivates your audience to act on your message. The external indicators of an enthusiastic delivery include a clear, strong voice; a crisp pace; and vocal emphasis on what you are saying. Enthusiasm is difficult to fake if you really are not excited about your presentation, so try to communicate only messages that you really believe in. Otherwise, give a different message or convince yourself that what you have to communicate is important or necessary or both. If you do not, your enthusiasm might seem phony to the audience.

Show Empathy. Another important characteristic of your verbal delivery is the empathy you have for your audience. Empathy is the care you have for the audience: your concern for understanding them, wanting them to hear what you have to say, answering their questions, and generally helping them in whatever capacity possible as a speaker. Like enthusiasm, empathy is difficult to fake and perhaps even harder to develop if it does not exist. You must convince yourself that members of the audience are much like you and are truly interested in what you have to say. Try and imagine what it's like to be sitting in the audience listening to your presentation. Try to see things from the audience's perspective!

Show Your Personality. As you become more experienced and comfortable as a speaker, more and more of your personality will come through in what you say. Personality is revealed in the manner in which you speak, in your style of delivery. Your personality shows through in the way you word your ideas and in the ideas you choose to share. If you interject personal examples—even if they are embarrassing or show a mistake you made—or asides as you would in conversation, your presentational style will contain more personality.

Your personality also is evident in a presentation if you appear to be enjoying what you are doing. We tend to be more likely to take risks and expose our personalities when we are having fun. You can also view this characteristic as the ability to be intimate with a crowd, to say and have confidence in saying what comes to mind as you deliver your presentation.

Control Your Volume. If you can't be heard, you can't be persuasive. If you have any doubt as to whether your audience can hear you, ask them when you begin your presentation. If you need to be louder, use greater force in your voice coupled with the support of a larger column of air. Practice speaking in an empty room; speak so that you can be heard in the farthest corners of the room. Even if you are small and have a quiet voice, you can learn to increase your volume without feeling as if you are straining your voice.

By varying your volume you can control the attention of the audience. Speak louder and slower during key phrases in the opening, main points, transitions, and conclusions. Increasing volume adds emphasis to what you are saying. You can also attract the audience's attention by reducing your volume: everybody wants to know what you are whispering. Try bringing your voice to just above a whisper and you will find that most groups become more attentive. This technique is used by many professional speakers to draw the audience to the speaker and keep them hanging on every word. It is a good technique to use when a group gets too noisy during a discussion.

Control Your Speaking Rate.   Your speaking rate should also be varied. People can usually understand words spoken at a rate of up to four times faster than in typical conversation, so don't be afraid of going too fast. If you are speaking quickly, make sure you occasionally slow down so that your words don't fly right past the audience. It is important not to speak too slowly because your audience will either tune out or lose patience. The best thing to do is to vary your rate, speaking faster when less important information is being communicated and more slowly to emphasize information. Or interject pauses during faster delivery to highlight points. Either of these methods will alert the audience that you are moving to a new point or emphasizing a point and they should listen more carefully.

Vary Your Pitch.   Pitch is the variation of your tone of voice. As with volume and rate, varying your pitch enhances your presentation and keeps you from speaking in a monotone. It is easy to practice varying your pitch in everyday conversation. In this way you can determine your range of pitch and work on using the entire spectrum available to you.

Select Your Words Carefully.   You should make your language appropriate to the situation and the group you are addressing. The most common mistake people make is to use words that are unfamiliar to the audience. If you use a term that is specific to your topic or industry, define it if you suspect any of the audience does not understand it, or use a more common term to explain the same point. Avoid slang or inappropriate language, including profanity. Some speakers swear to give emphasis to their points or to display their power, but swearing is seldom necessary to achieve these purposes.

Pronounce Your Words Correctly. Be sure to correctly pronounce the words used in your presentation. A mispronounced word, especially if it's a common word, is very annoying to members of an audience. When in doubt, look up the word, ask someone else, or use a different word.

Enunciate Clearly. Speak clearly and distinctly so that you are properly understood. The most common speech mistakes in this category are dropping the endings of words ("comin'," "hopin'," "meetin',") slurring your speech, mumbling, speaking with your mouth half-closed, and trailing off at the end of sentences. These problems are most common among speakers who are shy or feel inadequate in the role of speaker. Audiences are also quickly turned off by poor or inarticulate diction, so you should pay particular attention to this factor if it is a problem for you.

Poor enunciation can be corrected by increasing the amount of energy to your lips, mouth, and jaw, and controlling those muscles with more precision. Before a presentation many speakers repeat the vowels, *a, e, i, o, u,* and *y,* vary their emphasis, muscle movement, and rate of speaking each time until they feel that their mouths are warmed up. The same drill can be done with the entire alphabet or with tongue twisters. With each, open your mouth as wide as possible and exaggerate all movements. Drills like these, when practiced every day, have been known to produce noticeable improvement in only a week or two. Or you may opt to try what ancient Greek orators tried when poor diction was a problem, speaking with your mouth full of pebbles!

Use a Conversational Tone. This point cannot be emphasized enough! Avoid the overly formal, stuffy tone of a speech that is cluttered with passive verbs and long-winded phrases. Keep what you are saying in the active voice and directed specifically to those in the audience. Such a style will make your presentation sound extemporaneous and fresh rather than memorized or read. A conversational tone will also make your presentation easier to listen to and understand.

Watch Out for These Verbal Flaws. There are a variety of verbal flaws that can mar a presentation. One is simply the repetition of any single word at the beginning or end of sentences: "also," "and," "next," "so," or "well," are the biggest offenders. These words call attention to themselves and audience members may listen for them and perhaps start to count the times the word is used. A similar flaw is interjecting "ah" or "um" between thoughts.

Avoid these errors by learning to become comfortable with silence. You do not always have to be saying something; your speech will be more effective if you pause when mentally grabbing for your next

Watch Out for Your Ums and Ahs!

words. Practicing pauses when you practice your presentation will help. Writing the verbal crutch in large letters in the margin of your notes will serve as a reminder of what to avoid. Once you catch yourself using these unnecessary words, you will be well on the way to eliminating them.

If you catch yourself making a verbal slip or a grammatical error, don't emphasize your mistake, Don't grimace of fret or spend too much time attempting to correct the error. Instead, say the right word or repeat the phrase with a minimum of attention to the fact that you made a verbal mistake. Treat the slip very casually, perhaps by giving a slight smile as you continue. Do not speed up or say something like "What I meant to say was . . ." Keep your pace steady and think more closely about what you are saying so that another error does not soon follow.

Nonverbal Communication

Between 60 percent and 90 percent of all interpersonal communication is nonverbal. Your audience will decide whether they trust what you are saying based primarily on your nonverbal signals. You can check these findings easily by conducting your own experiment. The next time someone asks you a yes-or-no question, verbally reply one way and nod your head the opposite way. Ask your questioner which answer seemed dominant. Here are some nonverbal considerations to keep in mind when giving your presentation.

Don't Forget to Smile. One of the most effective means of projecting a confident image, increasing trust, and getting your audience to like you is to smile. Smiling is one of the few universal means of communication. Using a smile will help put your audience at ease and make your message more convincing. Try it, even if you don't feel like smiling.

Make Eye Contact. Even more important than smiling is the quality and quantity of your eye contact. Eye contact has been closely linked to perceived sincerity. One study attributes 38 percent of all audience perceptions of a speaker's meaning solely to the speaker's eye contact. Your eye contact should be steady, not darting from side to side or up and down, which increases mistrust. You should focus on each member of the audience several times in the course of your presentation. Finally, you should avoid looking excessively at your notes, at the floor or ceiling, or out a window or door.

One effective technique that is easily incorporated into your delivery style is to look an individual member of the audience in the eye until you have completed your thought, and then move on to another person. With practice, this technique makes for a very smooth delivery style that lets the audience feel you are communicating in a very personal manner, and makes you feel more at ease because you are talking with individuals. Our natural tendency in relationships of some distance is to look away while we are speaking and then back to a person when we are finished. The closer the relationship, the more eye contact will be made. By using eye contact with your audience you are signaling that you consider them friends.

Use Gestures.   Gestures are important for adding emphasis to your points and keeping your audience interested in what you have to say. Some gestures may seem unnatural or forced to a novice speaker, but they are effective tools in a presentation. Arm movements, head nods, and facial expressions are all examples of gestures you should be using. They are easily tapped by observing the gestures you use in one-on-one conversations and simply amplifying those same movements for a

Smile and Look Audience Members in the Eyes.

group situation. Another technique is to "break" the space around you when you are practicing your delivery, by swinging your arms and stretching them over your head. Then try to incorporate that same range of movement into your practice presentations: pointing, holding your arms out, numbering points with your fingers, covering your head, and so on. Some gestures will seem more natural for you and those are the ones you should use extensively.

Don't practice or plan to use specific gestures when you make specific points, for this will appear staged and will thus lose its effectiveness. Instead, practice gesturing in general. You'll find that gesturing serves as an excellent release for nervous energy as well.

How about your hands? Where do they go? If you leave your hands at your sides the option of gesturing remains, but if this feels too awkward to you, place one hand in your pocket and the other in front of you, holding your notes if necessary.

Walk Around. Walking is an effective way to control the attention of the group. Move closer to individuals whose interest you seem to be losing, or move away from the front of the room to encourage audience discussion. You can come across as more casual (and make yourself feel more relaxed) by walking in front of the lectern and sitting on the edge of a table as you speak. What you want to avoid is walking in a set pattern. If you do this, you will be seen as pacing, which is distracting to an audience.

Watch Out for Your Mannerisms. We all create little distractions of one type or another as we speak. Many are minor bad habits that we may not even be aware of. Playing with a pencil, your hair, or your notes, adjusting your clothes or glasses, or scratching are all examples of distracting nonverbal mannerisms. Watch for them and stop yourself when you start fidgeting.

KEEPING THE AUDIENCE WITH YOU

Probably all of us are afraid that we'll lose our audience during the presentation—that they'll start yawning or daydreaming. There are several things you can do to keep the audience awake and interested in what you have to say.

Speak with the Audience

You will always keep an audience more interested if you project an image of talking with them and not at them. You need to develop a sense for when the audience is with you and when they are not. Watch for clues from their facial expressions, eyes, and non-verbal behavior. If they look like they're about to fall asleep, you probably are not getting through! Experienced speakers sometimes use the analogy of a wave when talking about the concept of having the audience with you: your thoughts and ideas flow out over the audience, and you draw back a response to your words.

If you find uncertainty in the audience's response, you need to present the same information in a different way (a story, an example, more data) until the message is clear to the group. Imagine you are speaking *for* the group as you speak *to* them!

Avoid Rambling

As you describe your points be sure not to over-elaborate or you will lose your audience. Once you sense that the audience understands your point, do not continue with another example just because it comes to mind or you were planning to give more. Don't distribute a handout and then proceed to read the information from the handout to the group. This kind of behavior insults your audience and should be avoided.

Regain Their Attention

Don't let it get to you if the audience's attention drifts during your presentation. Do something different and unexpected. Ask a question or ask for questions, change your location in the room, or take a brief break, if appropriate. Another trick is to use the names of individuals in the group: "Now, John, I know you're probably saying . . ." or "Jackie has told me on several occasions that the department could expand operations if it were to . . ."

USING HUMOR

Humor has many advantages in a presentational setting, including lifting spirits, attracting attention, releasing tension, and getting people to like you. It can be one of the key elements of a great delivery if it is used correctly. Unfortunately, it is often used incorrectly by presenters. Speakers will cut down their own jokes, use inappropriate humor for the occasion, or simply not be funny. Here are some ways to avoid making those same mistakes.

Let the Audience Know When They Are Supposed to Laugh

It's not that you want to beg for a joke, but many times an audience is unsure if it is proper to laugh. No one wants to laugh at a statement that was meant to be serious, and if you have a dry wit or a believably sarcastic tone, you may at times leave the audience guessing. Be careful if you introduce humor for the first time late in your speech. The audience will probably not be expecting you to be funny and most likely will miss the humor. You can subtly introduce your humor with a disclaimer such as "A funny thing happened as I was preparing this presentation. . ." or "An example will make my point clear in a humorous way . . ."

Be Sure Your Humor Is Funny and Appropriate

Use humor that has been successful in other presentational settings, or test it on a group of coworkers. Humor needs to be appropriate for the situation and the audience. Inappropriate humor includes jokes that are sexist or racist. Also make sure the humor fits your style of delivery or it probably will not work. It is, by the way, fine for you to laugh at your own jokes—if they are good.

Tie Your Humor to the Content of Your Presentation

It is important to connect your humor to the rest of what you have to say; otherwise, it will appear that you are just making random jokes. You can accomplish this by using a clever transition from the joke to your content, such as "That joke may seem funny, but our topic today is not," or "You might be surprised as that person in the joke before I have finished today, because I have some startling facts to give you."

A second way to tie humor to your content is called "pulling a switch" by comedians and comedy writers. With this method you take a joke and change the character, subject, setting, or all three to make the humor more relevant to the speaking situation. Suppose you have a line such as "Finishing school is where you learn how to say 'fantastic' instead of 'baloney.' " You can introduce a character by referring to the person who introduced you as speaker.

> I showed John some of my notes on what I planned to say today and he kept repeating "fantastic, fantastic, fantastic." I finally asked him if it was really good and he told me . . .

Or you can apply the line to the subject of the presentation:

> I showed my manager the policy changes we'll be discussing today and all he could say was "fantastic" . . .

Or the setting may be changed:

> We've all dealt with the customer. I followed one sales representative on his rounds last week and was impressed at how positive he always was. Regardless of what business we were at, or who he was speaking to, he kept interjecting the word "fastastic" into the conversation. Finally, at the end of the day, I asked him . . ."

Humor can be a powerful tool for controlling the speaking situation. Learn its subtleties and you will be very fortunate. Pay attention to others who are funny to see what specifically they are doing. Practice your jokes over and over and vary your emphasis, timing, and gestures to see what works the best. Start to keep a log of humor you hear that you like and that will fit your personal style.

CLOSING YOUR PRESENTATION

Here are some tips for making sure your presentation ends on the right note.

Avoid Going Overtime

Pay attention to the time! Wear a watch or have someone signal you when time is running out. If you do anticipate going slightly past your allotted time, do so only with the permission of the group. For instance, ask the audience how they would prefer to spend the remaining time. "We have about five minutes remaining. I can give a few more examples of how the new rate changes affect the typical customer, or I can take a few questions. Are there any questions?"

Don't Pack Up While You Are Talking

You want to end with a bang, not fizzle out. Do not start bunching your notes or gathering your audiovisual aids while you are still making points. Your audience will do the same, the noise level in the room will increase, and no one will be listening.

End on a High Note

Make your memorable, prepared closing remarks, pause with a smile and look to the audience, and briskly take your seat. Do not lower your energy and confidence level until well after you have stopped. Avoid saying "Thank you." Even if you made mistakes and came nowhere near convincing your audience, a professional will keep up that professional image. Keep smiling and tell yourself that next time will be even better!

Don't Leave Your Notes or Audiovisual Aids

As a courtesy to the next speaker, if there is one, quickly remove all of your materials. This also keeps a subsequent speaker, who may be presenting an opposing view, from making use of your visual aids.

HANDLING QUESTIONS

Most presentational situations allow members of the audience to ask questions. Good answers to the audience's questions enhance the effectiveness of your speech. If you handle yourself with authority and confidence, the audience will remain convinced of your message. If you know your topic well, this is an excellent chance for you to show that fact. If, however, you become uneasy or unconvincing in answering straightforward questions about your topic, the effectiveness of your entire presentation may be jeopardized. At this time you can tailor your message to the specific needs of individuals in the audience. In order to come across as professionally as possible, use the following guidelines when answering questions.

Repeat or Rephrase the Question

This gives you a chance to organize your thoughts and make sure you clearly understand the question.

Don't Get Defensive When Answering Questions. Handle
Questions with Authority and Confidence.

It is also a courtesy to those members of the audience
who may not have heard the question. For example: "Your question then is, How significantly will
our forecasts be affected? Is that right?"

Compliment Tough Questions and Questioners

Everyone likes to be flattered, and complimenting
audience questions helps to get individual audience
members on your side as well as to defuse any hostility on the part of the questioner. So when an audience member asks you a question, respond with,
"That is a very good question which brings up an

important point. . . ." Be careful not to compliment every question; if you do, you will seem insincere.

Frame Your Answer

Qualify your response so that it does not contradict any other information you have already presented. If the question raises other concerns that you believe are relevant, discuss those topics as well, but be sure not to drift too far from the original question or you might forget to answer it! An example of framing your answer is "The best I can tell you, given the data we have available, is . . ."

Answer the Question Clearly

Make sure that you specifically address the individual's question. If, for example, it was a yes-or-no question, be sure to specifically answer "yes" or "no," regardless of whatever additional information you use to buffer your answer. If you don't know, say so, but offer to find out. Answer a question whenever possible, but don't bluff information you are not sure about. For example: "That's an excellent question that I don't have an answer to. I could find out the answer, however, and get back to you later today."

Check the Clarity of Your Answers

If you have any doubts at all as to whether you answered a question satisfactorily, make sure you ask, "Did that answer your question?"

Keep Control of the Presentation

Serve as the gatekeeper during question-and-answer periods, monitoring the length of questions and replies and the amount of interaction that takes place between audience members. For example, if an individual disagrees with your reply and proceeds to argue with you, interrupt him or her. Offer to discuss the topic further after the group adjourns, or state, "Let's try to get as many questions as possible. I see a few more hands so let's hear from some others right now . . ." You should also cut short and summarize rambling questions.

Your attitude toward the audience's questions in large part determines how well you answer them. If you view questions as though audience members are trying to put you on the spot, you are bound to become defensive with your answers. If you approach the questions, instead, as an indication that audience members are interested in what you have said and want further clarification, then the time you spend answering them helps to sell the audience on your ideas.

POLISHING YOUR PRESENTATION

Go over the following techniques for polishing your presentation and check off those you need to work on. Then run through another practice of your presentation and try out some of the things you have checked.

1. Things to do to get your message across

    a. Communicate with pictures and analogies   _____

    b. Number your points   _____

    c. Emphasize your organization   _____

2. Techniques of good verbal communication

    a. Show enthusiasm   _____

    b. Show empathy   _____

    c. Show your personality   _____

    d. Control your volume   _____

    e. Control your speaking rate   _____

    f. Vary your pitch   _____

    g. Watch your wording   _____

    h. Watch your pronunciation   _____

    i. Watch your enunciation   _____

    j. Use a conversational tone   _____

    k. Watch out for repeated words
       (ahh, umm, so, well, next . . .)   _____

3. Techniques of good nonverbal communication

    a. Don't forget to smile   _____

    b. Use eye contact   _____

    c. Use gestures   _____

    d. Walk around   _____

    e. Watch out for distracting mannerisms   _____

4. Techniques for controlling the audience

    a. Speak with, not at, the audience   _____

Continued.

     b. Avoid rambling   _____

     c. Regain the audience's attention   _____

5. Techniques for using humor

     a. Let the audience know when they are
        supposed to laugh   _____

     b. Check the appropriateness of your humor   _____

     c. Tie your humor to the content of your
        presentation   _____

6. Ways to conclude on a positive note

     a. Avoid going overtime   _____

     b. Don't pack up while you are talking   _____

     c. End with a smile and briskly take your seat _____

     d. Don't leave your notes and visual aids   _____

7. Techniques for answering questions

     a. Repeat or rephrase the question   _____

     b. Compliment tough questions   _____

     c. Frame your answer   _____

     d. Check the clarity of your answers   _____

     e. Keep control of the presentation   _____

8

On the Day of Your Presentation

When the day of your presentation arrives, you will want to act and think differently to help mentally psych yourself up for the approaching event. Let's consider the time from when you first wake up on the day of your presentation to the moment when all eyes turn toward you as you are introduced as the next speaker.

STAYING CONFIDENT

No matter how many times you've practiced, you may start losing some of your confidence when the day of your presentation arrives. Let's look at some tricks for keeping up your confidence.

Greet the Day with Anticipation

It may sound corny, but springing out of bed and saying "My big day!" rather than groaning and rolling over to escape reality for a few more moments may well set the tone for the day. You need to be "up" for a quality delivery, and this will be easier to accomplish if you begin the day at an energetic level. Thinking and saying positive things to yourself does affect your mental disposition and level of confidence, so try it! Make up statements that you are comfortable with, or choose from these examples:

- "I really feel prepared for this presentation; I'm glad I'm doing it."
- "That audience is going to be impressed. They are going to learn a lot they don't know."
- "This presentation should actually be fun. I'm planning to enjoy giving it."

Do Something Special

Another way to make yourself feel mentally and physically better is treat yourself in some way during the day. Make a small purchase of an item—perhaps on a whim, when you see something you like in a store. Have favorite foods for breakfast or lunch. Call a friend you haven't spoken with for some time. Compliment someone you work with. Any positive activity you do that is out of the ordinary will more than likely have a positive effect on you.

Go Through One More Practice

Even if you have practiced your presentation a thousand times, you'll find that it helps your confidence to run through a practice run one more time on the day of your presentation. Go ahead, make some time and practice—you'll find it is worth it!

Wear Favorite Clothes

As long as it is appropriate to the speaking situation, you should choose an outfit you feel comfortable in for your presentation. Your clothing should be a notch nicer than that of your audience. When in doubt, dress more formally to show you have respect for the situation, the audience, and your position as a speaker. Avoid any sharp changes in your appearance, such as a haircut, on the day of your presentation; you might feel overly self-conscious!

Arrive Early

Plan to be at the site of your presentation at least an hour before your audience arrives. Come even earlier if you have a variety of audiovisual aids or equipment to check. Use the checklist at the end of this chapter to check all the preliminary arrangements. To make it just a little more familiar and comfortable for you when you begin, spend a few moments at the lectern or the spot from which you will be speaking.

Check Your Introduction

Talk with the person who will be introducing you to see if he or she has enough information about you and the topic. Make suggestions as to what information might enhance your credibility or build the interest of your audience.

JUST BEFORE YOUR SPEAK

When you are called on to speak, you enter a different world. Even though it may seem unfamiliar at first, facing a group may be one of the most rewarding experiences you will ever have.

Relax While You Wait

If there are speakers or other agenda items prior to your presentation, focus your attention on staying relaxed. Take slow, deep breaths and stretch any muscles that start to become tight. Avoid thinking about your speech content other than the words you plan to begin with. If you are relaxed, focus on the other activities going on in the room.

Don't Make Any Changes

Avoid the tendency to make last-minute changes and "improvements" to your presentation, especially in your introductory remarks. Changes at this stage are apt to confuse you and may throw off your delivery. This does not include a spontaneous introduction that is an extension of your introducer's remarks. If you think of a good spontaneous introduction that fits the situation, go ahead and use it!

Listen Closely to Your Introduction

See if you will need to add to or correct what the introducer is telling the audience. For many in your audience the introducer's comments will be all they know of you and will thus determine their expectations of you.

Spring from Your Seat

Get the attention of your audience in a direct, assertive way by snapping out of your seat and briskly approaching the lectern. The confidence and authority you emit will enhance your credibility. Your energy level will be contagious.

Greet the Audience

If you are up at the podium waiting for audience members to enter the room (say, at a conference), then from the moment the first audience member enters the room, pretend you are "on stage." Act as if all attention is focused on you, even when it is not. Then, in a short while when all attention does become focused on you it will not seem so disruptive. Try to establish physical contact with and individually meet each member of the audience prior to your presentation. The purpose is to make them as familiar to you as possible. Your initial contact will also help to dispel any possible hostility or animosity from group members. People tend to be less critical of those they know and like, and your initial contact can help to establish that rapport.

Minimize Prespeech Activities

Your audiovisual aids should all be in place and set to go. Ideally you should have your notes already placed at the lectern in a stiff folder, or carry such a folder up with you. Avoid having to hunt for and unfold notes taken from your pocket. If there is not a lectern, keep your notes in your hand or on a nearby table. Avoid having to move objects or the lectern to a different location. Such activities only distract from your presentation. If you need to make a change, do so before you say anything, or you might end up fumbling with a microphone for several minutes into your presentation.

Wait for the Audience's Attention

Many speakers, especially if they are nervous, prefer to charge right into their presentation, even if the group is not listening to them. Avoid this tendency. Instead, look out at the audience, moving your eyes from one side of the room to the other, and wait for all to be looking at you. If several members of the group are chatting they will quickly stop when they observe you are looking at them.

Pause and Begin

When you have the attention of the group, start your presentation in a loud, clear voice, using the exact wording that you practiced and focused on while you were seated. You should not have to glance at your notes to begin speaking, especially if your opening remark is a phrase such as "It's a pleasure to be here." Do not begin with an apology of any type, particularly for being unprepared.

Wait for the Audience's Attention Before You Begin.

AND NOW, LADIES AND GENTLEMEN, YOU'RE ON! PRELIMINARY ARRANGEMENTS CHECKLIST

Go through this checklist the day of your presentation to make sure everything is in order when you go to deliver your presentation.

Session _____

Date & Time _____ Room _____ No. Expected ___

SEATING ARRANGEMENT

Auditorium _____ Classroom _____ Informal _____ U-Shape _____
Other _____

ROOM AND SUPPLIES	Satisfactory	Not Needed	Needs Attention
Chairs			
Tables			
Lighting			
Ventilation			
Distractions			
Ashtrays			
Pencils/Scratch Paper			
Name Cards			
Coffee/Soft Drinks/Water			
Handouts			
Electrical accessories (bulb/cord/plug/extension)			

Continued.

Audiovisual equipment

Supplies (chalk/eraser/
felt pens/grease pencil/tape)

Audience notification

9

Evaluating Your Presentation

Without fail, the minute you sit down you will remember something else you meant to say. Don't let it concern you. Most of us feel we could have done better in a presentation and we can usually identify several factors that would have contributed to a higher quality presentation, such as more practice, more information, more time, and so on. All speakers are faced with those same constraints, and to bring them up before, during, or after your presentation will just seem like excuses to members of your audience. Avoid using any kind of excuse during your presentation: "We've been undergoing a lot of changes so I'm glad I was even able to pull this together."

THE REACTIONS

Now it is time to give yourself some feedback. Let's first analyze your reactions to your presentation, and then the audience's reactions.

What Did You Think?

Perhaps the best evaluation of a presentation is made by the presenter. As the presenter, you know best what obstacles were present. Before you analyze any of the reactions from other people, try to identify a few items that you felt went exceedingly well and a few that could have gone better. This initial evaluation can then serve as a basis for gathering more feedback from others; that is, you can check your perspective—especially in the areas of improvement—against the perspectives of those in the group.

What Did Your Audience Think?

As you speak with members of the audience, you will probably find that most of the comments you receive are positive. Accept those comments with gratitude, but press for a more detailed reaction to what could have been better. Every presentation can be improved, and if you don't find out how your presentation could be improved, chances are you will not do better the next time. If you know some of the members of the audience, have them complete an evaluation form such as the one included at the end of this chapter.

Did You Achieve Your Purpose?

Usually any reaction at the end of a presentation is referred to as a "happiness rating." You will receive only general comments about how good a job you did and how pleased the members of the audience are with what they heard. Usually it is worthwhile to go through a more thorough evaluation that examines what actually changed as a result of your presentation.

Will members of the audience think or act differently as a result of your presentation? Did you achieve your purpose? These questions are not always easy to answer. Behavior changes might not be noticeable until a person's next opportunity to act on the topic. For example, if your presentation was on changes in office procedures, you may not know if the group understood and will follow the changes until they have an opportunity to do so. Perhaps they indicated that they understood your points, but when the time comes to use what they learned they may be confused. They might then ask someone else in the department to come to see you for clarification. If in the latter case your goal was to keep everyone in the department from coming to you for an explanation of the new procedure, your goal may have been only partially reached. If, however, your goal was to have members of the department stop using the old procedure, regardless of how they obtained information about the change, your presentation can be viewed as more successful.

MAKING CHANGES BASED ON YOUR EVALUATIONS

Let's look now at how you are going to improve your next presentation. Read the following sections and write down a list of things you did right and a list of things you would like to do differently. File your list away for your next presentation!

What Would You Do Differently?

If you were to give the same presentation again (which is quite possible), what would you do differently? What exactly have you learned from this experience? Unless you pursue and follow up on answers to these questions, you will not be the most effective speaker you can be. That is, your style will stagnate, and although giving presentations may become easier for you, you will not become a better speaker. Give the matter some thought and make a list of specific changes to make in the preparation and delivery of your next presentation.

What Presentational Skills Do You Want to Develop?

In addition to the specific changes you plan to make for your next presentation, consider how you would like to improve generally as a speaker. Perhaps you want to develop a stronger voice, make better use of humor, use more and better quotations, or focus on being more enthusiastic and dynamic. Select one or two areas for your general development and develop a strategy for improvement. Your strategy may include joining a speakers group such as Toastmasters International; obtaining additional speaking references such as a joke book, or practicing specific speaking skills, such as articulation exercises. Set estimated time frames for each goal to increase your commitment to achieving each one.

Practice, Practice, Practice

Once you know the "rules" and have developed a satisfactory "formula" for giving a presentation (such as the one presented in this book), you need only practice to become an accomplished speaker. Look for opportunities to use your skills, no matter how formal or informal the setting. Speak up at social gatherings, within your family, at staff meetings, even in elevators or on the bus! Come to relish the opportunity to "say a few words," and when presented with a formal opportunity to speak ("Would you be willing to speak to our staff about . . ?"), learn to automatically respond, "I'd love to!" With that attitude, in only a short time you will be a truly professional speaker!

ABBREVIATED PRESENTATION
EVALUATION FORM

Presenter _____ Date _____
Presentation Title _____
Audience _____ Location _____
Purpose _____
_____

1. Did the speaker achieve the intended purpose? Why or why not?

2. What was the best about the presentation?

3. What could have been improved in the presentation?

4. What were the speaker's best presentational qualities?

5. What presentational skills could the speaker improve on?

6. What did you learn from the presentation?

7. What will you do differently as a result of hearing this presentation?

10

Special Speaking Situations

This chapter discusses some special speaking situations you might find yourself in during your professional career. You will find insights in this chapter about how to make each opportunity a success.

INTRODUCING A SPEAKER

At some point you will be faced with the responsibility of introducing another speaker. This does not sound very intimidating, yet not very many people are skilled at this relatively simple assignment. A good introduction incorporates the following steps.

Welcome and Introduction

As the introducer, you have the responsibility of warming up the audience for the speaker. You should first welcome the group and take a moment or two to establish a rapport with the audience. Then, discuss the purpose of the meeting, the topic of the presentation, and why that topic is important and relevant. Many times a speaker will write his or her own introduction and will want it read, as is, without any changes. A good introduction for a speaker should include the following steps.

Speaker's Qualifications

Without mentioning the speaker's name or pointing out the person, mention his or her impressive, relevant qualifications for presenting information on the topic.

Speaker's Name and Title

When the audience's interest is at a peak, conclude your introduction with the name of the presenter and the title of his or her presentation. "Help me welcome _____ speaking today on _____. Lead the applause, and continue it until the speaker reaches the front of the room. Shake hands with the speaker and leave the room on the side opposite that used by the speaker; that is, do not cross in front of or in back of the speaker.

IMPROMPTU PRESENTATIONS

An impromptu presentation is a situation in which you have little or no warning that you will be called on to speak and so you are essentially unprepared. It is a scary situation even for experienced speakers.

Let's look at how to make these situations easier to handle.

Prepare

Although there are several unknowns in the typical impromptu speaking situation, it is still possible to prepare for one. First, try to predict when you might be called on. Often, if others know you are knowledgeable about a topic, they are apt to ask for your opinion. For example, if you are going to a staff meeting and one of the agenda items is next year's budget, and you have been collecting data on that topic, it is a safe bet that you will be asked to contribute to the conversation. Or, if you are an avid runner and the group you are in is discussing physical fitness, you may well be asked about your beliefs and practices.

Fortunately, in most situations in which we are asked to speak without warning, it is because someone else believes we are knowledgeable on the topic. Even if we are not, we will seldom be asked for facts and figures, but rather for our opinions and ideas— and it is possible to have an opinion about anything.

Another technique for preparing is to always have some stories or speaking strategies ready. Save your note cards from previous presentations and capsulize the information, or carry a trinket that can easily be converted into a story. Some professional speakers carry a coin that has a favorite saying or motto on it applicable to a wide range of topics, for example, a quotation about trust. When called on to speak, they begin with the quote and show the coin, and then explain how the topic is relevant to the present situation. Their stock but impressive opening gives them a few extra minutes to determine what to say next.

A similar approach is to automatically begin an impromptu talk with a personal story of something that recently happened to you, perhaps that same morning. Then, as you are speaking, determine how you can twist your story to apply to the topic at hand. This may seem difficult, but with some practice you will quickly become skilled. The following are two impromptu organization formats that can be adapted to almost every situation.

Take a Stand and Defend It

As you are rising to speak, grab onto the first logical idea that crosses your mind, pause once you are standing, and begin with a clear specific position on the topic. Support your contention with any of the devices discussed earlier in this book, such as a story, an item from the newspaper, or something you heard from a friend. After you have backed up your claim with two or three bits of support, come full circle, repeat your initial position, and sit down. Some individuals believe that if you start and end a talk in a decisive or clever manner (such as returning to the same story you began with, adding a new twist), it doesn't matter what you say in between.

Past, Present and Future

The other standard format that you can usually count on for an effective impromptu presentation is to organize your information in a chronological manner. Start with the past, how the situation being discussed has come about. Explain the present: what is being done now. And offer a plan for the future—what should be done to correct, resolve, or change the situation.

Once you overcome any shyness during impromptu speaking you need to be careful not to abuse the privilege that comes with this opportunity. Speakers often ramble, or get off the subject, or needlessly repeat themselves. When you have completed what you have to say, sit down!

THE AFTER-DINNER SPEECH

Whether it is an awards banquet, an out-of-town business meeting, or a social affair, many speakers will eventually have an opportunity to present an after-dinner speech. The tone of such an occasion is casual and light. The audience has just completed a meal and (hopefully) enjoyed some good fellowship. The stage is set for the evening to continue in an informal, entertaining way, with you the speaker as leader. Don't make the mistake of thinking that entertaining is easy and end up boring your audience. Instead, follow these tips.

Be Entertaining

Enliven the audience with stories and humor. Be good-natured and plan to enjoy your presentation. Use variety to help hold the audience's attention. For example, use different types of humor: puns, witty phrases, personal embarrassments, or stories with unusual twists. Use vivid speech to describe events and keep an exciting, enthusiastic tone throughout your delivery. If you use several jokes, be sure they relate to a theme that is relevant to the speaking situation.

Be Positive

Uplift your audience by being optimistic about your topic of discussion. Do not be too serious or discuss negative problems or situations in depth. Don't attack the audience's beliefs or attempt to arouse them over a specific cause. Audiences want and expect a much lighter presentation at such an affair.

Be Simple

Keep your points clear and direct. Do not discuss abstract issues unless you employ a number of concrete examples for ease of understanding. Keep the number of points to a maximum of two or three. Use simple, conversational language.

Be Brief

Attention is difficult to hold when audience members have full stomachs and have been sitting for some time. Plan on speaking ten to fifteen minutes, and then allow the group to take a break. Having to sit much longer will jeopardize the patience and attention of your audience.

HANDLING THE HOSTILE AUDIENCE

One situation that you should be prepared for is knowing how to handle an audience that is hostile—perhaps openly hostile—toward you, your topic, or the situation. Ideally, you can identify potential hostility in the audience analysis conducted during your preparation, and thus be better prepared to handle it. Even if hostilities are not detected in advance, here are techniques to try if you are ever faced with a hostile group.

Clarify the Hostility

As soon as you detect any hostility, try to determine why it is there. If possible, ask the person who made a hostile comment for further explanation of his or her viewpoint. Otherwise you may inadvertently continue to offend members of the audience or to alienate them.

Emphasize the Similarities

Try to identify and expand the points of agreement between you and those who disagree with what you are saying. Focus on how the two sides are similar. Emphasize how much you are like them in whatever ways this might be true.

Work Objections into Your Presentation

If you are reasonably sure that an objection will be raised by members of the audience, bring it up first in your presentation. "Now, I know there are those present who disagree with the planned proposal. I understand their position and hope they will understand why this proposal will benefit their cause. Specifically, there are three reasons . . ." Or, better yet, directly cut off an objection by stating: "There is one possible objection I want to answer right now so that no one will bring it up when I'm finished, and it concerns the phase-in period . . ." It will take an especially gutsy audience member to later bring up the same objection. Other members of the audience are likely to think, "Wasn't that guy listening?"

Don't Get Personal

If you do get into an argument, focus on the topic, not the person. Avoid responding in a similar manner to emotional outbreaks or personal jabs at your character. Remember that you have the higher level of authority as speaker in this situation. You will lose credibility in the situation if you stoop to an unprofessional level.

Use Humor as a Release

An appropriate joke can help to relieve tension for you and the audience. Do not, however, use humor to discount the audience's concerns or make a joke at their expense.

Admit When You Are Wrong

If at all possible, when you have made a mistake and a member of the audience has corrected you, admit that an error was made. Your honest, open attitude will gain you support from other members of the audience, and your credibility will increase when you do stand your ground.

CHECKLIST FOR INTRODUCING A SPEAKER

1. Welcome
   _____ Welcome the group
   _____ Establish rapport with the group
   _____ Discuss the purpose of the meeting
   _____ Introduce the topic of the presentation and why it is relevant

2. Speaker's Qualifications
   _____ Build up the audience's interest by discussing the speaker's qualifications without letting the audience know who the speaker is

3. Speaker's Name and Title
   _____ Introduce the speaker by name and title
   _____ Lead the applause for the speaker

CHECKLIST FOR IMPROMPTU PRESENTATIONS

1. Be Ready for Anything
   _____ Try to predict when you will be called on to speak
   _____ Always have some stories or speaking strategies ready

2. Option 1: Take a Stand and Defend It
   _____ Grab on to the first logical idea that crosses your mind
   _____ Pause when you are standing, and begin with a clear and specific stand on the topic
   _____ Support your contention with a story, something you read in the newspaper, or something you heard from a friend
   _____ After you have backed up your claim with two or three bits of support, come full circle, repeat your initial position, and sit down

3. Option 2: Past, Present, and Future
   _____ Start with the past and discuss how the situation has come about
   _____ Explain the present and discuss what is being done now
   _____ Offer a plan for the future—what should be done to correct or change the situation

Index